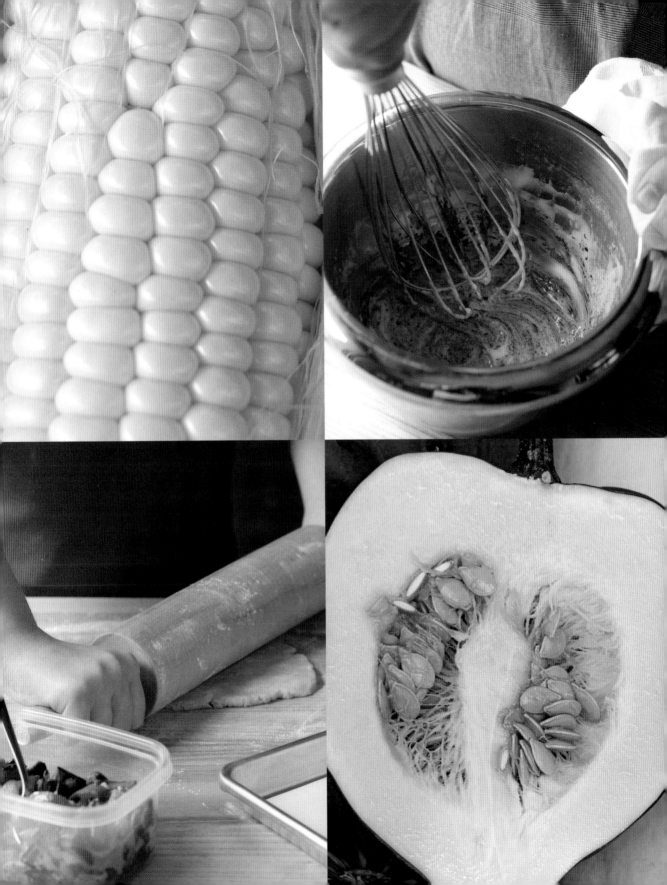

cooking

a seasonal guide to the pleasures of

MARK ERICKSON, CMC *and* LISA ERICKSON
THE CULINARY INSTITUTE OF AMERICA

Photography by Ben Fink

LEBHAR-FRIEDMAN BOOKS
NEW YORK • CHICAGO • LOS ANGELES • TOKYO

for one

preparing delicious meals for yourself

LIBRARY OF CONGRESS CATALOGING-IN-PUBLICATION DATA

Cataloging-in-publication data for this title is on file with the Library of Congress.

ISBN 978-0-86730-822-8

THE CULINARY INSTITUTE OF AMERICA

President: Dr. Tim Ryan '77

Vice-President, Dean of Culinary Education: Mark Erickson '77

Senior Director Continuing Education: Susan Cussen

Director of Publishing: Nathalie Fischer

Editorial Project Manager: Mary Donovan '83

Editorial Assistant: Erin Jeanne McDowell '08

LEBHAR-FRIEDMAN BOOKS

A company of Penton Media, Inc.

249 West 17th Street, New York, NY 10011

Publisher: Maria Tufts

Art Director: Kevin Hanek

Manufactured in Thailand on acid-free paper

table of contents

CHAPTER THREE

Fall 65

CHAPTER TWO

Summer 31

CHAPTER FOUR
Winter 105

introduction

For countless americans living on their own, cooking for one is a fact of daily living. Far from dreading it, many people find it to be a satisfying, fun, rewarding activity—not just a chore. It's a way to get back in touch with a familiar rhythm of daily living. The pleasure of seeking out the best ingredients, preparing them to their own preferences, experimenting with new flavors and ingredients, and the sensory pleasures of cooking—the feel of chopping something, the sound of foods sizzling in a wok, the aroma of a simmering soup— are as important to their sense of well-being as daily exercise is.

Keeping your meals flavorful, interesting, satisfying, and healthful is the goal of this book. The strategies and recipes we've developed put to rest any negative connotations about cooking for one person. It does not have to be a pot of soup served all week long or one roast chicken showing up at every meal. Dinner should not mean "leftovers." Rather, by careful planning, paying attention to the seasons, and following some basic cooking techniques, one can enjoy a delicious and healthy meal even on a busy weeknight.

Through our "his-and-hers" strategies, we share our ideas and (sometimes differing) opinions. We offer suggestions for planning and a host of tips to make cooking easy and efficient and enable you to get dinner on the table, not just once a week, but night after night. The varied and, we think, exciting recipes reflect our travels and affinity for interesting and fresh flavors.

The ideas in this book are not simply theory. We are both practitioners in the art of cooking for one. Mark has honed his skills by dint of living a bi-coastal life for nearly 15 years. He spends most of his weekdays in an apartment in upstate New York. With our daughter now in college, Lisa has recently joined the ranks of single cooks. Although our cooking styles differ and our separate lo-

cations and schedules influence the choices in our meals, we both share the same passion to eat well and the determination to do just that.

Home is in Georgia, where we enjoy gardening almost year-round. Our vegetable and herb gardens are small but bountiful. Our yard also supplies us with a variety of fruits for summer eating and storage. But our passion for food extends beyond that. Over the

years our travels have taken us around the globe. No matter the locale, we can usually be found shopping and cooking from the seasonal markets. Whether we are on a culinary tour of Asia, spending the summer in Napa Valley, or renting a *gîte* in France, be assured we are reveling in the pleasures of the table.

Single cooks sometimes skip the "extras" like vegetables or a salad. We've developed a number of dinners that incorporate a main course and a side dish or two that add very little in the way of extra work or time, but that do add greater variety for meals that are healthier and more satisfying.

Here are the three elements of our cooking-for-one strategy:

- *Adopt a food lifestyle* Take the time to make cooking and eating dinner an integral part of the day.

- *Sensible cooking* Include fresh flavors, interesting textures, and varied ingredients to make meals more satisfying and healthier.

- *Use practical strategies* There are a host of suggestions in the mise en place chapter as well as throughout this book, ranging from advance prep work to storage tips.

We hope this book will open your eyes to a whole new way of cooking for yourself.

– Mark and Lisa Erickson

equipment and tools

Y OU DON'T NEED a lot of tools, just the right tools—sharp knives, good pans, and a few hand tools. Good tools, large and small, make it possible for a cook to prepare any dish well.

Pots and pans are constructed from a variety of materials. Different metals conduct heat with varying speed and evenness. **Copper** transfers heat rapidly and evenly. It is also heavy, expensive, and requires significant time and labor to maintain its appearance. Since copper will react with food, copper pans are generally lined with a nonreactive material like stainless steel or tin. **Aluminum** is widely used to make pots and pans; it is highly reactive with foods and is sometimes anodized to prevent the soft metal from turning foods gray. **Cast iron** holds heat well and, once seasoned, can be virtually nonstick. Since iron pans will pit and rust without proper seasoning, many are coated with enamel to simplify care. **Stainless steel** is a relatively poor conductor of heat, but it is nonreactive and easy to maintain. Copper or aluminum is usually sandwiched between stainless steel layers to combine good heat conduction with easy care.

Nonstick coatings have become popular for their convenience. Although they are not as sturdy as metal linings, they offer convenience and require less fat or oil in cooking.

Pans used in the oven are produced from the same basic materials as pans for the stove top. They can also be made from more delicate materials, such as earthenware, glass, or ceramic, since oven heat is less intense than the direct heat of a burner. Shiny surfaces reflect some heat away from the food and slow the cooking process, which helps prevent foods containing large amounts of fat and sugar from burning. Dark surfaces, on the other hand, hold heat better for well-developed crusts and deeper color. If a recipe calls for placing a pan on the stove top as well as in the oven, make sure that it is both flameproof and ovenproof.

The pots and pans we use most often include these:

- **Sauce pans** are basic pans with straight or slightly flared sides with one long handle. A 1½-quart pan is perfect for making one or two portions. **Sauce pots** are often larger and they often have two loop handles and a lid. We use a 5- or 6-quart pot to make stock.

- **Sauté pans** are wide, shallow skillets. Our most used sauté pans measure 6 or 10 inches.

- **Dutch ovens,** also known as flameproof casseroles or simply casseroles, have sides that are as high as, or only slightly less high, than the pot is wide. You can use these casseroles right on the burner as well as in the oven. They typically have a domed lid. The size we reach for most often is a 2½-quart casserole.

- **Baking dishes and roasting pans** are heavy, rectangular pans with medium-high sides. A roasting rack is a good item to have. Ceramic casserole dishes are also useful; we find that 1½- to 2-quart capacity dishes and pans are the most useful for single cooks.

- **Soufflé dishes** are round, deep, ceramic dishes with straight sides to guide the rising soufflé. **Ramekins** are small, round dishes, usually made of ceramic or earthenware, for baking and serving individual portions. **Gratin dishes** are typically flat with shorter sides than a soufflé dish; they may be round or oval, with or without lids, and made of ceramic, enameled cast iron, or enameled

steel for baking and serving. We generally use a 6- to 8-ounce size dish to make single gratins and soufflés.

- We like to use a **pizza stone** for making pizza and flatbread. These ceramic "stones" go into a cold oven to preheat along with the oven.

TOOLS

In the process of preparing a meal, a cook may measure, weigh, strain, and mix ingredients numerous times. A well-equipped kitchen will have tools that allow quick, simple, and accurate preparation of food. A basic collection includes:

- Tools for measuring, including **measuring cups, measuring spoons,** and an accurate **kitchen scale.**

- Hand tools for mixing, including **mixing spoons, whisks, spatulas, tongs,** and **ladles.** Mixing bowls come in a wide range of sizes and materials; a set of two or three bowls is really all you need.

- **Instant-read thermometers** monitor changes in the temperature of food as it cooks and help determine doneness.

- Hand tools for prep work including **vegetable peelers** (useful for peeling vegetables as well as shaving Parmesan or chocolate) and graters, whether you prefer a 4-side box grater or microplanes. **Melon ballers** are helpful when you are coring apples to stuff and bake, or to cut fruit for salads. **Kitchen shears** are useful for performing a wide variety of tasks in the kitchen—from cutting twine to snipping herbs to cutting up a small bird.

- To strain, drain, sift, and purée foods, you need a **sieve** made from fine mesh. A **colander** is useful for quickly draining foods such as pasta or blanched vegetables. **Food mills** purée soft or cooked foods. Resembling a pot or sieve, they have a curved blade at the bottom that rests flat against a perforated disk. A set of disks offers a range of textures, from coarse to fine purées.

- We use a **blender** and a small **food processor** to purée foods or to mix doughs. A **mortar and pestle** is good to have for making a traditional pesto.

KNIVES

A good set of knives is a worthy investment. Knives are used more than any other piece of equipment in your kitchen.

- **Chef's** or **French knives** are used for a wide variety of cutting tasks from chopping to mincing to slicing. Their blades, most commonly 8 to 10 inches long, taper from a sturdy heel that can cut through small bones to a thin tip that slices delicate items smoothly.

- **Utility knives** are smaller versions of the chef's knife. Measuring 5 to 7 inches, they are useful for lighter cutting chores.

- **Paring knives,** with their 2- to 4-inch blades, are used for peeling and trimming vegetables and fruits.

- **Boning knives** have narrow, sharply pointed blades that offer good maneuverability for separating raw meat cleanly from bones.

- **Filleting knives** are similar in shape and size to boning knives, but have thin, flexible blades for cutting between the more delicate flesh and bones of fish.

- **Mandolines** are slicing devices that cut vegetables quickly and conveniently. A Japanese-style mandolin may have interchangeable blades for slicing, julienning, or making other cuts. The blades may be adjusted to change the thickness and shape of cuts.

mise en place

Probably our most important strategy is something chefs refer to as "mise en place," which means having things at the ready. Traditionally, this would involve assembling and prepping ingredients before the actual cooking begins. In our case, we are applying the term to the entire process of bringing meals to the table—from menu planning to shopping strategies to prepping the ingredients. As all chefs know, mise en place is the key to running an efficient and successful kitchen.

MENU PLANNING

The first step in menu planning is deciding what you want to cook. Everything else flows from that, including shopping. We've organized our recipes by season and offer a range of dishes—from soups to sandwiches, pizza to polenta, stews to succotash—because the foods that are fresh and in season are the foods that most inspire us. That said, when planning a weekly menu,, we also keep in mind a few techniques to help us buy efficiently and avoid waste.

Healthy cooking matters to us so we use the list and menu plan as helpful tools to encourage us to include more fruits, vegetables, and nuts in our meals. We choose healthier proteins for our meals and emphasize fish, poultry, nuts, and legumes. We look for healthier carbohydrates like whole or minimally processed grains.

- Plan meals that use up perishable ingredients in a variety of recipes. This principle is easy to follow by eating seasonally.

- Use substitutes. Throughout the book we give ideas for substituting ingredients. Like many people, we don't always have, or want to buy, every ingredient listed in a recipe. We often

	BREAKFAST	LUNCH	DINNER	PREP/OVERS
MONDAY	*TRAVEL*	*TRAVEL*	*Chèvre soufflé with broccoli salad*	*Cook pot of oatmeal*
TUESDAY	*Oatmeal with dried fruits*	*Lunch with client*	*Sausage and fig skewers*	*Bake fig gratin, soak black beans*
WEDNESDAY	*Fig gratin with Greek yogurt*	*Sausage sandwich*	*Straciatella, baked apple*	*Simmer pot of black beans*
THURSDAY	*Oatmeal with apples*	*Lunch with client*	*Cornish game hen, black bean sauce*	*Freeze extra beans (save some for Friday breakfast)*
FRIDAY	*Black bean burrito*	*TRAVEL*	*TRAVEL*	*TRAVEL*

Taking a moment to plot out the week's meals makes shopping efficient, and helps ensure that you'll have everything on hand that you need when you're ready to cook. The chart above shows a real-world example of a typical week.

On Monday, prepare a soufflé from the freezer (our recipe makes enough to bake one and freeze one for later) and put a pot of oatmeal on to make enough to have for two breakfasts. It reheats quickly in the microwave. On Tuesday, use some of the figs for the skewers and bake a simple gratin for breakfast the next day. Make enough sausage to use in a sandwich for Wednesday's lunch. Soak some black beans overnight. On Wednesday, breakfast and lunch are already made. Put the beans on to simmer for Thursday night's dinner. On Thursday, finish the oatmeal and make the Cornish game hen. Friday is a travel day; make a simple black bean burrito from the leftover beans cooked on Wednesday.

use substitutes to vary a recipe or move it into the next season. We love to try new flavors and ingredients, keeping meals interesting.

- Have a plan and a backup. Our mulligan meal strategy, for the times when life catches us by surprise or we find we have bits of this and that to use up. That's when we turn to our well-stocked pantries and freezers where we keep the basics for putting together a quick and healthy meal, for instance, pasta with broccoli or soup made with chicken stock and white beans from the freezer.

SHOPPING STRATEGIES

To make a good shopping list that gets you through the whole week, use a menu template like Mark's (see the example on the previous page) to develop a menu plan. Give careful thought to generating prep-overs; they make efficient use of your time.

This can mean partially preparing foods one day and finishing them another. It can also mean doubling a recipe so it's part of dinner one night, and the basis for another meal the next day. Multi-tasking helps to keep the time spent in the kitchen to a minimum.

- Assemble your shopping list with amounts noted

- Check your pantry for staples and adjust your list

- Scan the newspaper to clue in on what's in season and what's on sale

Develop a healthy pantry and keep it stocked with flavorful and interesting ingredients and staples. You'll find items like orange blossom water, fish sauce, tahini, soba noodles, dried chipotle flakes, rice noodles, olives, and walnut oil in our recipes. We love exploring new flavors and specialties from around the world. We keep the following on hand:

- A variety of dried pastas and beans

- Canned tomatoes

- Canned tuna

- Tea

- Baking items including flours, sugars, cocoa powder, and baking chocolate

- Canned beans

- Canned stock

Take your list to the store with you and use it—but don't be afraid to grab an unexpected opportunity (white peaches at the height of the season, a great deal on fresh tuna, and so on). When you get home, batch process foods before you store them to make mealtime prep go faster and cut down on clean up.

Wash and dry lettuces and herbs and store them loosely covered in plastic bags or containers. Peel onions and garlic and leave whole. Half and seed peppers and store in plastic. Peel and cut carrots and celery for lunches, snacks, or salads. Juice lemons or oranges if needed for a recipe later in the week.

Repackage bulk items like nuts or grains into smaller, airtight containers. Cut larger steaks or fillets into portions, wrap them well, and store them in the refrigerator if you plan to cook them in a few days, or in the freezer for longer storage.

Use your recipe's ingredient list the way a professional uses a mise en place list: peel, chop, and measure all of your ingredients before you start cooking. Then, once you start, you won't be interrupted or distracted.

Multi-task while you are cooking when you can. Fit in some prep work; for instance, put some garlic into the oven to roast while you are baking or roasting something else. Plan ahead for other meals; in other words, make planned-overs like these: a pot of oatmeal or rice, a pot of beans, a doubled batch of ratatouille. These foods don't demand much in the way of constant attention.

Make your own "convenience" foods, like the ones in the list at the right. We also freeze tomato sauce, sliced peaches, whole blueberries, and peach pies, too, but we can usually only do this in the summer when we have a little extra time. Managing the overflow from the garden is a lot of work, but worth it when winter sets in!

THE REFRIGERATOR

Most foods go right into the refrigerator, but, as noted above, we do some processing on a few items before we store them, especially greens and herbs. Six things we always have in our refrigerators are: Greek yogurt, Parmesan, milk, seasonal fruits, salad greens, and dressings.

THE FREEZER

We use our freezer more than we used to because it is a great way to store some of the basics that help us to cook better and more efficiently. When you freeze small quantities they thaw quickly, too. Here is a list of what you are likely to find in our freezers:

- Homemade Chicken Stock, p. 134

- Pizza Dough, p. 142

- Pâte Brisée, p. 143, Quick Puff Pastry, p. 143

- Leftover braising liquids to use for sauce

- Tomato Sauce, p. 134

- Mark's Pesto, p. 141

- Ginger root

- Nuts (almonds, walnuts, pecans, pine nuts, and hazelnuts)

- Grated cheeses (the last bit of Fontina or cheddar, for instance)

- "Leftover" canned items like coconut milk, tomato paste, or diced tomatoes

- Pancetta or prosciutto slices

- Cooked legumes like chickpeas or black beans

- Icebox Cookies (baked or unbaked), p. 133

CHAPTER ONE

Spring

the spring pantry

WHILE FEBRUARY GIVES way to March, you'll still find carrots, winter squash, celery, potatoes, parsnips, and turnips in the markets coming from cold storage, along with onions, apples, and garlic. When spring arrives (March in Georgia, but not until late April or early May in New York) the produce section starts to change. What's in season during spring? Here are some springtime favorites:

Apricots (late spring)

Artichokes

Arugula, mâche, watercress, and other tender salad greens

Asparagus

Fava beans

Fennel

Fiddlehead ferns

Fresh peas (shell peas, snow peas, and sugar snap peas)

Leeks and ramps (early)

Mushrooms, notably morels

New potatoes

Radishes

Rhubarb

Spinach

Spring onions, green onions, and scallions

Strawberries

HERBS are usually easy to find year-round, but the herbs that first raise their heads in gardens on the East Coast are these:

Chives

Mint

Parsley

FISH AND SEAFOOD also have seasons. We look for these species in spring:

Cod

Halibut

Shrimp

Soft-shell crab (late spring)

stracciatella

THIS IS TRULY a meal in minutes—perfect for busy days. Stracciatella is surprisingly substantial, and the recipe is easy to double or triple, making it a good dish for nights when you have a guest or two.

LISA: I became a complete convert to the value of a good homemade stock while writing this book, and now I don't think I'll ever go back. If you have stock in the freezer, you can thaw it in the microwave while you whisk together the egg and Parmesan cheese.

MARK: Good planning should always leave room for a little innovation. That's why a big part of my weekly plan is leaving a slot for a "mulligan meals." This soup is a good basic platform that you can vary easily. No spinach on hand? Skip it. Traditional recipes don't call for it at all, but we like the addition.

1 egg

2 tbsp finely grated Parmesan

1¼ cups Homemade Chicken Stock (page 134)

1 cup chopped fresh spinach (about 2 oz)

Salt and freshly ground pepper as needed

Grated Parmesan to taste

1. Crack the egg into a small bowl. Add the Parmesan and 2 tablespoons of the stock. Whisk until evenly blended. Set aside.

2. Bring the remaining stock to a boil over high heat in a small saucepan. Turn the heat down to medium and pour the Parmesan-egg mixture into the stock while whisking constantly. Continue to whisk the soup as it comes back to simmer, about 1 minute.

3. Remove the soup from the heat and add the spinach, stirring until it has wilted and turned a deep, vibrant green, less than 1 minute. Taste and season with salt and pepper, if necessary. Serve in a heated soup plate with additional grated Parmesan to taste.

asparagus salad with crispy prosciutto

THIS EASY APPETIZER salad is at its best when the asparagus is crisp, bright, and in season. It is quick to make and should be tossed together just before serving. The quantities for the salad dressing make more than a single salad serving, so save any extra dressing to use on salads or as a marinade for chicken or fish.

MARK: Slender asparagus looks pretty, but the best flavor is found in more substantial stalks. If you have a choice, opt for thicker asparagus.

LISA: If you've never tasted crisp, raw spring asparagus, you are in for a revelation. Use a mandolin or Japanese slicer, if you have one, to cut the asparagus very thin.

1 tbsp finely chopped shallots

2 tbsp lemon juice

Salt and freshly ground pepper as needed

1 slice prosciutto or pancetta

3 tbsp extra-virgin olive oil

½ tsp grated lemon zest

8 spears asparagus, peeled and sliced thin on the diagonal

½ oz Parmesan, shaved into curls with a vegetable peeler

1 tbsp pine nuts, toasted

1. Place the shallots in a small bowl with the lemon juice, a pinch of salt, and a few twists of freshly grated pepper. Let the shallots macerate for 15 minutes. (This will reduce any harsh bite in the shallots.)

2. Sauté the prosciutto in a dry, nonstick sauté pan over medium-high heat until crisp and browned on both sides, about 1 minute on each side. When it is cool, tear into irregular pieces and reserve.

3. Add the olive oil and lemon zest to the shallots and lemon juice. Whisk until the dressing is slightly thickened and well-blended. Add the sliced asparagus and toss to coat evenly.

4. Mound the asparagus on a plate, scatter the prosciutto and Parmesan pieces over the top, sprinkle with the pine nuts, and serve.

black pepper and fennel crusted salmon with a spinach and orange salad

LISA: An aromatic spice crust adds flavor and texture to salmon. The contrasting textures and temperatures add to the whole experience. We suggest soaking red onion slices in ice water to tame the sometimes sulfurous bite of the onion. If you buy a large piece of fish, one that weighs 8 or 9 ounces for instance, prepare the entire piece and save whatever you don't want for dinner tonight to serve in a salad the next day or add it to a Salad Wrap (page 71).

MARK: If you've followed our advice about mise en place and have already cleaned and spun dry your greens for the week, you have very little work ahead of you. Or, use this night's prep time to clean enough spinach to enjoy over the next three or four days.

BLACK PEPPER AND FENNEL CRUSTED SALMON

THE FLAVORS IN the crust are a great match for salmon, but they would also work with sea bass or halibut. You can use aniseeds instead of fennel seeds; the flavors are similar.

¼ tsp whole black peppercorns

¼ tsp whole fennel seeds

1 piece salmon fillet (about 5 oz)

½ tsp olive oil, plus as needed for searing

Salt as needed

1. Heat a small sauté pan over medium heat. Add the peppercorns and fennel seed, swirling the pan to keep the spices moving, until the spices are aromatic, about 30 seconds. Pour the spices into a mortar and pestle and pound until the spices are coarsely ground.

2. Rub the salmon fillet lightly with ½ teaspoon olive oil, sprinkle with salt, and press the ground spices evenly over the top of salmon. Set aside.

3. Add a few drops of olive oil to a small, nonstick sauté pan and heat over medium heat. Add the salmon, crusted side down, and cook without disturbing until a golden brown crust forms, about 3 minutes. Turn the salmon and cook to your preferred doneness (an additional 4 minutes for medium).

SPINACH AND ORANGE SALAD

1 orange

4 cups spinach

½ cup shaved fennel

2 or 3 thin slices red onion, soaked for 15 minutes in ice water and drained

1½ tsp red wine vinegar

¼ tsp Dijon mustard

2 tbsp olive oil

Salt and freshly ground pepper as needed

1. Cut the orange into segments, working over a bowl to collect the segments and the juices as described on page 142.

2. Combine the spinach, fennel, red onion, and orange segments in a salad bowl.

3. In a small bowl, whisk together 2 teaspoons of the reserved orange juice, the red wine vinegar, and the mustard. Add the olive oil and whisk to blend and slightly thicken the dressing. Taste the dressing and add salt and pepper, if needed.

4. Add the dressing to the salad and toss until the spinach is evenly coated. Top with the salmon and serve at once.

MEDITERRANEAN NOODLE CAKE

THIS LIGHT AND healthy one-dish supper is the perfect vehicle for improvisation and experimentation. The simple topping recipe made with cool, crisp vegetables adds an interesting contrast of temperatures and textures that we really enjoy, but the dish would be equally good with a sauté of spring vegetables.

LISA: After making this a few times, you will want to start experimenting with your own toppings and fillings. If you don't have the herbs we suggest, then simply use whatever herbs you have in the refrigerator or growing in your garden: basil, thyme, fresh oregano, marjoram, or chives.

MARK: The pasta for the noodle cake can be cooked and chilled a day or two in advance, or better yet, make a little extra pasta at a previous dinner to save yourself a step.

TOMATO-CUCUMBER TOPPING

¾ cup quartered cherry tomatoes

¼ cup diced cucumber

1 tbsp extra-virgin olive oil

Zest and juice of ¼ lemon

1 tsp chopped dill

1 tsp chopped shallots

Salt and freshly ground pepper as needed

Pinch sugar

NOODLE CAKE

1 tsp olive oil, divided use

1⅓ cups cappellini, cooked al dente (2 oz dry pasta)

½ cup coarsely chopped spinach or arugula

⅓ cup crumbled feta cheese

2 scallions, chopped

1 tsp chopped dill

1. Mix the ingredients for the topping together and set aside to allow the flavors to develop while you make the noodle cake.

2. Heat ½ teaspoon of the olive oil in a small, nonstick sauté pan over medium heat. When the oil is hot, add half of the cappellini and press it into a cake about ½-inch thick. (The thickness of your cake matters, so if you are using a pan that is a little too large, scoot the noodles to one side of the pan to make an evenly thick, round cake.)

3. Top the noodles with the spinach or arugula, feta, scallions, and dill. Top with a layer of the remaining noodles. Press down on the noodle cake with a spatula to seal the filling in between the layers. (Spinach and arugula will shrink as they cook.) Cook until crisp and brown on first side, 3 to 4 minutes.

4. Turn the cake over onto a plate. Return the pan to the heat and let it get hot. Add another ½ teaspoon oil and when the oil is hot, slide the cake from the plate into the pan, browned side facing up. Finish cooking on the other side until it is brown and crisp, another 3 to 4 minutes.

5. Cut the noodle cake into wedges and transfer to a plate. Spoon the topping over the wedges and serve.

asian-style chicken and peanut noodles

LISA: The Asian ingredients in this dish are usually available at most larger supermarkets, if they are not already on your pantry shelf or in your refrigerator. If you like the idea of the dish but don't have soba noodles, substitute whole wheat noodles (thin spaghetti or vermicelli are good). Whole wheat pastas have plenty of texture and flavor and are a good match for this sauce. Even a regular pasta would work in a pinch. Whatever type of noodles you choose, remember to reserve a cup of the cooking water to use in preparing the sauce.

MARK: The flavors in the peanut sauce are a good match for shrimp or pork, as well as chicken. We like this dish both hot and cold and often make a double batch. The colors aren't as vibrant the next day, but it is still delicious.

2 oz soba noodles (Japanese-style buckwheat spaghetti)

1½ tsp sesame oil

4 oz skinless, boneless chicken thigh meat, cut into thin strips

¼ cup chopped scallions

1 tsp minced garlic

2 tsp finely chopped ginger

½ cup thinly sliced red pepper

½ cup snow peas or sugar snap peas, cut in half on the diagonal

1 tbsp peanut butter

1 tbsp soy sauce

1 tsp rice vinegar

½ to 1 tsp chili garlic sauce, to taste

1 tbsp chopped cilantro

GARNISH OPTIONS

Thinly sliced scallion greens

Coarsely chopped roasted peanuts

1. Bring a medium pot of salted water to a boil. Cook the noodles, following directions on the package. Reserve 1 cup of the pasta water and drain. Rinse the noodles with cold water to stop cooking and then let them drain. Set aside.

2. Add the sesame oil to a wok or skillet and heat over medium-high heat. Add the chicken and cook, stirring until opaque and cooked through but not brown, about 2 minutes. Remove to a plate.

3. Add the scallions, garlic, and ginger to the wok and stir about 30 seconds until fragrant. Add the red pepper and cook another 30 seconds. Add the snow peas and then the peanut butter and soy sauce; stir well. Add ½ cup of the pasta cooking water to the pan, stirring until creamy. Add the vinegar and chili garlic sauce. Stir in the reserved chicken and noodles and mix well, adding more pasta cooking water if needed to make a saucy consistency. Add the chopped cilantro.

4. Spoon into a heated pasta bowl and top with chopped scallion greens and a sprinkling of chopped peanuts.

SAVORY BREAD PUDDINGS

SAVORY BREAD PUDDINGS are great as a main dish, with a salad for dinner, or they can be served as a side dish with grilled or roasted meat. They are similar to a quiche, but much easier to make for one person.

A savory bread pudding has three basic components: the bread, the custard, and the flavoring or filling. The type of bread used can vary, but should complement the filling. For instance, a light, summery tomato pudding is best when made with a simple baguette. A heartier bread, such as sourdough or whole wheat, can be matched with more robust flavors such as mushrooms, rosemary, and olives.

The custard is made by whisking together egg yolk, cream, and milk. The cream helps the custard to maintain its silky texture, though it is possible to slightly vary the proportions of milk, cream, or half-and-half, using what you have in your refrigerator.

BLT BREAD PUDDING

FRESH TOMATOES CAN release liquid as they cook. That extra moisture could affect the texture of the custard, so we blot them first: Lay the tomato slices between two layers of paper toweling and set aside for a few minutes.

CUSTARD

1 egg yolk

2 tbsp heavy cream

¼ cup whole milk

Salt and freshly ground pepper as needed

3 slices baguette, about ¾ inch thick (1 oz)

FILLING

½ tsp olive oil

½ cup thinly sliced onion

½ cup coarsely chopped arugula

2 or 3 thick slices plum tomato, quartered and blotted dry

1 slice bacon, cut into ½-inch pieces and cooked until crisp

2 tbsp grated cheddar cheese

1. Preheat the oven to 350°F. Lightly butter a 6- to 8-ounce shallow gratin or baking dish.

2. Make a custard by whisking together the egg yolk, cream, and milk with a pinch of salt and pepper. Add the bread slices, turning to saturate both sides, and then set aside to soak while you prepare the vegetables.

3. Heat the oil in a skillet over medium heat. Add the onion and cook, covered, until softened and just barely golden, about 3 minutes. Uncover, add the arugula, and toss until wilted, about 2 minutes. Remove the skillet from the heat and stir in the tomato and the bacon pieces.

4. Lift the bread slices from the custard and make alternating layers of bread with the onion-arugula-tomato mixture in your gratin dish. Pour the remaining custard over the top of the assembled pudding. Sprinkle the top with the cheddar cheese, and then let the pudding rest for 10 minutes before baking.

5. Bake until the pudding is browned and puffed, and a knife inserted in the middle comes out clean, about 25 minutes. Let the pudding rest 5 to 10 minutes for the best flavor and texture.

MUSHROOM-LEEK BREAD PUDDING

CUSTARD

1 egg yolk

1 tbsp cream

5 tbsp whole milk

1 tsp Dijon mustard

Salt and freshly ground pepper as needed

3 slices sourdough baguette, about ¾ inch thick (1 oz)

FILLING

½ tsp olive oil

½ leek, cleaned and cut into thin ribbons

3 cremini mushrooms, trimmed and sliced thin

½ tsp minced garlic

¾ tsp chopped thyme

1 tbsp white wine

½ cup coarsely chopped fresh spinach

2 tbsp grated Parmesan or Gruyère

1. Preheat the oven to 350°F. Lightly butter a 6- to 8-oz shallow gratin or baking dish.

2. Make a custard by whisking together the egg yolk, cream, milk, and mustard, and a pinch of salt and pepper. Add the bread slices, turning to saturate both sides, and set aside to soak while you prepare the vegetables.

3. Heat the olive oil in a small skillet over low heat. Add the leek and stir to coat with oil. Cover the skillet and let the leek cook until tender, but without any browning, about 4 minutes. Add the mushrooms, garlic, thyme, salt, and pepper, and cook, uncovered, stirring from time to time, until the mushrooms are browned, about 5 minutes. Add the wine and let it reduce slightly, about 1 minute. Add the spinach and cook until wilted, another minute. Remove the pan from the heat.

4. Lift the bread slices from the custard and make alternating layers of bread with the mushroom-leek mixture in your gratin dish. Pour the remaining custard over the top of the assembled bread pudding. Sprinkle the top with the cheese, and then let the pudding rest for 10 minutes before you put it in the oven.

5. Bake until the pudding is browned and puffed, and a knife inserted in the middle comes out clean, about 25 minutes. Let the pudding rest 5 to 10 minutes for the best flavor and texture.

fish souvlaki

LISA: If you are a fan of the traditional meat souvlaki, we think you will find this lighter version equally satisfying. We like mahi-mahi for its meaty texture and rich flavor, but any firm fish will work for this dish, just as long as it is thick enough to be cubed and will hold together while it grills.

MARK: Warming your flatbread is a good touch. If you are grilling, wrap the bread in foil and put it along the edge of the grill to warm and soften. If you are using a broiler, put the wrapped bread on the bottom rack of the oven below your broiler pan.

SOUVLAKI

4 oz mahi-mahi or other firm fish

2 tsp lemon juice

1 tsp olive oil

½ tsp chopped fresh oregano or ¼ tsp dried

Salt and freshly ground pepper as needed

One 6-inch pita bread or other flatbread
   (naan, lavash, etc.)

Cucumber-Yogurt Sauce (follows)

⅓ cup shredded romaine lettuce

1. Cut the fish into 1-inch cubes. Whisk together the lemon juice, oil, oregano, salt, and pepper. Add the fish to the mixture and toss to coat the fish well. Set aside to marinate at room temperature while you preheat the grill, about 30 minutes.

2. Preheat a broiler or grill. Remove the fish from the marinade and thread it on a metal or bamboo skewer. Wrap the pita bread in foil.

3. When grill or broiler is hot, grill the fish over direct heat, turning to cook it evenly, about 2 minutes on each side. While the fish is cooking, warm the pita in foil on edge of grill until soft and heated through.

4. Place a sheet of parchment paper, slightly larger than pita, on work surface. Unwrap the pita and place it on the parchment paper. Spoon the yogurt sauce over the pita. Remove the fish from the skewer and place on top of sauce. Top with lettuce. Using parchment paper, wrap the sandwich tightly into a cone shape and serve.

CUCUMBER-YOGURT SAUCE

GREEK YOGURT IS our preference for its richer, thicker texture. If you are using regular yogurt, let it drain through a coffee filter-lined sieve or colander for at least 30 minutes before using. The longer it drains, the firmer it gets. If you let it drain more than 1 hour, put it in the refrigerator so it doesn't spoil.

¼ whole cucumber

2 tbsp Greek yogurt

2 tsp minced onion

3 cherry tomatoes, quartered

½ tsp chopped fresh mint

½ clove garlic, finely minced

Salt and freshly ground pepper as needed

1. Peel and seed the cucumber, cut lengthwise into ½-inch wide strips, and then crosswise into very thin slices. Wrap it in a paper towel and squeeze out any excess juice.

2. Stir together the yogurt, onion, tomatoes, mint, and garlic in a small bowl. Add the cucumber and blend evenly. Taste and adjust the seasoning with salt and pepper.

grilled chicken with black bean sauce and mango salsa

LISA: This is a healthy, satisfying meal that requires no additional accompaniments. You can make the Black Bean Sauce a few days ahead of time to simplify dinner on a busy night. We prefer bone-in chicken when grilling because it stays moister.

MARK: The black bean sauce is very quick to prepare if you are using black beans that you've already cooked (page 136). Our recipe makes enough so that you can have the leftovers another day, thinned with a bit of stock and renamed "Cuban Black Bean Soup." Serve it topped with sour cream, chopped scallions, and cilantro, and add a green salad with a bit of diced mango and red onion (or any leftover mango salsa) and a piece of cornbread.

GRILLED CHICKEN

1 portion bone-in chicken breast (about 6 oz)

1½ tsp olive oil

1 tsp lime juice

½ tsp chopped garlic

Salt and freshly ground pepper as needed

½ cup Black Bean Sauce (follows)

2 to 3 tbsp Mango Salsa (follows)

1. Place the chicken breast in a zip-close bag. Add the olive oil, lime juice, garlic, and a bit of salt and pepper. Seal the bag and then massage the marinade into the chicken. Put it in the refrigerator to marinate for at least 30 minutes and up to one day.

2. Preheat a grill or broiler to medium heat (page 144). Grill or broil the chicken until golden browned and completely cooked through, about 5 minutes on each side, depending on the size and thickness of your chicken breast.

3. Warm up the black bean sauce, thinning it with a bit of stock or water, if necessary, and spoon it onto a heated plate. Place a chicken breast on top of the bean sauce, spoon the mango salsa over the chicken, and serve.

BLACK BEAN SAUCE

IF YOU'VE PREPARED the sauce ahead of time, reheat it gently in a saucepan over low heat or in the microwave. The sauce will thicken under refrigeration, so thin it with a bit of water or stock as you reheat it.

1 tsp olive oil

½ cup finely diced onion

¼ cup small dice green or red bell pepper

1½ tsp minced garlic

¼ tsp ground cumin

¼ tsp oregano

Pinch ground chipotle or crushed red pepper flakes

1½ cups cooked black beans (page 136)

1½ cups water or Homemade Chicken Stock (page 134)

½ tsp lime juice or as needed

Salt and freshly ground pepper as needed

1. Heat the oil in a medium saucepan over medium heat. Add the onion and sauté, stirring occasionally, until tender and translucent, 2 to 3 minutes. Add the bell pepper, garlic, cumin, oregano, and chipotle or red pepper flakes. Continue to stir over medium heat until the spices are aromatic and the pepper is tender, 1 to 2 minutes.

2. Add the beans and water or stock. Bring to a full boil, then reduce the heat to low. Simmer, uncovered, until the sauce has a good flavor and consistency, about 20 minutes.

3. Using a slotted spoon, transfer about one-third of the beans to a small bowl and mash to a paste with a wooden spoon or a fork. Return the paste to the pan and stir well to blend. Season with lime juice, salt, and pepper to taste.

MANGO SALSA

⅓ cup medium-dice mango

2 thin slices red onion, soaked in ice water for 15 minutes and drained

2 tbsp medium-dice red pepper

2 tbsp whole cilantro leaves

1 tsp chopped jalapeño (seeded)

1 tsp lime juice

Salt and freshly ground pepper as needed

Combine the ingredients in a small bowl and toss to combine. The salsa may be stored covered in the refrigerator for up to 2 days.

poached salmon "au printemps"

WE THOUGHT TWICE about using a French title for one of our recipes, but no other name suits this dish better than *saumon au printemps*, which means "salmon in the style of springtime." This dish reminds us of our love for French food, and celebrates the awakening of spring.

MARK: This technique for poaching salmon is virtually foolproof. Since most of the cooking happens off the heat, there's no chance you'll end up with overcooked salmon. By the time the fish has cooked, the poaching liquid has cooled down. You can leave the salmon directly in the poaching liquid as long as you need to.

LISA: Fresh peas are available for such a short time; I buy them as soon as I see them in the market and enjoy them in several meals throughout the week. I always cook the peas fresh each time and find that they are at their best served simply, perhaps tossed with a bit of butter and maybe some chopped fresh mint, chives, or basil. To make one of my favorite spring vegetable dishes, I sauté some shallots in a bit of butter and add the peas along with some sliced asparagus and a touch of water to cook the vegetables, and finish with some freshly chopped herbs.

POACHED SALMON

1 piece salmon fillet (about 5 oz)

Salt and freshly ground pepper as needed

½ tsp unsalted butter

1½ tsp minced shallots

1 sprig thyme

2 tbsp white wine

¾ cup Homemade Chicken Stock (page 134)

BEURRE BLANC

1 tbsp dry white wine

1 tbsp heavy cream

1 tbsp unsalted butter

½ tsp lemon juice

PRINTEMPS GARNISH

⅓ cup shelled green peas, blanched if fresh (see Note) or thawed if frozen

1 hard-boiled egg, peeled and cut into ½-inch dice

2 tsp chopped chives, cut into ¾-inch pieces

1. Season the salmon with salt and pepper and set aside.

2. Melt the butter in a small skillet over medium-low heat. Add the shallots and thyme to the skillet and cook, stirring, until the shallots are translucent, about 1 minute. Add the wine and stock and bring to a boil. Reduce the heat to low and simmer for 1 minute.

3. Turn the heat off and add the salmon. Cover the skillet and let the fish cook until it is just barely opaque in the center, about 5 minutes. Remove the fish from the skillet and set it on a warm plate, loosely covered to keep warm while preparing the beurre blanc.

4. To prepare the beurre blanc, return the skillet to medium-high heat and let the cook-

ing liquid reduce by half, about 4 minutes. Strain through a fine sieve. Return 3 tablespoons of the poaching liquid to the pan. Add the white wine and heavy cream. Simmer until reduced by half, about 2 minutes. Remove the saucepan from the heat and whisk in the butter, about 1 teaspoon at a time.

5. Taste the sauce and season with lemon juice, salt, and pepper. Add the peas, egg, and chives to the sauce and return the saucepan to very low heat to gently warm it. Place salmon in a deep plate and spoon the sauce over and around the fish. Serve immediately.

To keep the peas bright green, plump, and perfectly done, we take the extra step of cooling them off after they've been cooked just long enough to turn tender and a brilliant green. This step is something chefs call "blanching and refreshing" the vegetable. You can use it for most green vegetables including asparagus, broccoli, and green beans. Cook the vegetables in plenty of boiling salted water until their colors intensify and then drain them. Immediately put them into a bowl of ice water. That keeps them from overcooking and also maintains a beautiful green color. When chilled, drain once more. They are now ready to use in hot or cold dishes.

cod with oven-dried tomato pesto and a warm white bean salad with watercress

LISA: The scent of basil makes us imagine we are somewhere near the Mediterranean whenever we make this quick and healthy dinner. The pesto in this dish relies mainly upon the moisture in the oven-dried tomatoes to hold it together and has very little oil compared to most pesto recipes. The pesto recipe makes just enough for one meal, and it comes together in less than a minute. If you have a traditional pesto on hand, though, you can use it instead.

MARK: This salad really deserves the far superior texture and flavor of home-cooked beans. Dried beans can be soaked and cooked several days in advance, even frozen and thawed to use as you need them. Apart from this warm bean salad, I'll add beans to sautéed greens or soups, use them as the basis of a rich stew that can double as a sauce, or perhaps in a garlic-spiked purée to use as a dip or a spread.

COD WITH OVEN-DRIED TOMATO PESTO

TRY THIS RECIPE with other varieties of fish: tuna, grouper, and halibut are all equally delicious. The cooking time may vary according to the thickness of your fish.

1 cod steak (about 5 oz)

Salt and freshly ground pepper as needed

1 tsp olive oil

Warm White Bean Salad with Watercress (follows)

Oven-dried Tomato Pesto (follows)

1. Rinse the cod with cold water and pat it dry. Season the cod lightly on both sides with salt and pepper.

2. Heat the oil in a small nonstick skillet over medium heat. When hot, add the cod and cook without disturbing the fish until it is golden on the first side, 3 to 4 minutes. Turn the cod and finish cooking on the second side until just opaque in the center, another 3 to 4 minutes. (These cooking times may differ, depending upon how thick or thin your cod steak is.)

3. Serve the cod on the warm bean salad, topped with a spoonful of pesto.

WARM WHITE BEAN SALAD WITH WATERCRESS

1 cup cooked white beans (page 136), drained and rinsed

2 tbsp Homemade Chicken Stock (page 134)

½ cup coarsely chopped watercress

3 or 4 thin slices sweet or red onion, soaked in ice water for 15 minutes and drained

1 tbsp diced red bell pepper

½ garlic clove, finely minced

1½ tsp olive oil

1 tbsp lemon juice

1. In a small bowl, mash 2 tablespoons of the white beans with a fork until fairly smooth. Combine the mashed beans with the remaining whole beans and the stock in a small saucepan. Cook over low heat until they are warmed, but not boiling. Remove the pan from the heat and set aside.

2. Combine the watercress, red onion, red pepper, and garlic in a bowl. Add the bean mixture, drizzle with the olive oil and lemon juice and toss gently to combine and coat evenly. Check the seasoning and add salt and pepper if you like. Serve the salad while it is still warm.

OVEN-DRIED TOMATO PESTO

2 tbsp Oven-dried Tomatoes (page 141) or sun-dried tomatoes

½ tsp brined capers, drained and rinsed

4 large basil leaves

½ tsp chopped shallots

Olive oil, if needed

Salt and freshly ground pepper as needed

Combine all of the ingredients in a mortar and pestle and pound to a coarse paste. (If you don't have a mortar and pestle, mince the ingredients together and transfer to a small bowl.) Depending on the moisture content of your tomatoes, you may want to add up to 1 teaspoon of olive oil to create a creamy, sauce-like consistency. Add salt and pepper to your taste.

brazilian-style fish stew

MARK: This take on a traditional Brazilian fisherman's stew is a delicious melding of flavors: sweet coconut milk, briny seafood, fresh vegetables, and heat from the chiles. It is a great representation of many regional dishes in which the ingredients vary according to what's available at the market. After you've become comfortable with this version, feel free to experiment with other vegetables and seafood, letting your market basket and imagination guide you.

LISA: Serve this stew over steamed rice (page 136) accompanied by salad greens topped with mangoes or oranges and red onion tossed with Lemon-Garlic Salad Dressing (page 139). If you make steamed rice to enjoy with your Brazilian Fish Stew, make an extra portion or two to serve with another meal later in the week; it reheats beautifully in the microwave.

1 piece white fish filet (about 4 oz), such as tilapia, snapper, cod or halibut, cut into 1-inch cubes

3 medium shrimp, peeled and deveined

2 tsp lime juice

2½ tsp olive oil, divided use

1 tbsp chopped cilantro, divided use

1 tsp chopped serrano chile (seeded), divided use

1 tsp minced garlic

½ cup chopped onion

⅓ cup diced mixed red and green pepper

⅓ cup chopped tomato (peeled and seeded)

⅓ cup unsweetened coconut milk, lite or regular

⅓ cup clam broth

Salt and freshly ground pepper as needed

Steamed rice (page 136)

1 scallion, sliced thin on diagonal

1. Combine the fish and shrimp in a bowl and drizzle with the lime juice. Add 1½ teaspoons olive oil, 1 teaspoon cilantro, ½ teaspoon serrano, and ½ teaspoon garlic. Toss to coat the fish evenly. Cover the bowl and let the fish marinate for at least 30 minutes and up to one hour.

2. Heat 1 teaspoon of oil in a small saucepan over medium heat. When hot, add the onion and pepper and sauté, stirring frequently, until softened, about 4 minutes. Add the remaining garlic, the serrano, and the tomatoes. Cook over low heat until the garlic is fragrant, about 1 minute.

3. Add the coconut milk, clam broth, salt, and pepper and bring to a simmer. Cook until very flavorful, about 10 minutes, and then add the fish and its marinade and cook until just cooked through, about 3 minutes. Stir in the remaining cilantro just before serving. Spoon the stew over hot steamed rice, sprinkled with sliced scallion.

lemon and rosemary crusted lamb chops with fennel and artichoke salad

L AMB IS A TRADITIONAL springtime ingredient. Since it has a rich, robust flavor, it pairs well with the bold flavors of lemon and rosemary. Lamb chops are perfectly sized for the single cook. Replace the fennel and artichoke salad with the Asparagus Salad on page 5, if you prefer.

MARK: This recipe evolved during my days in California and I think it beautifully illustrates the fresh flavors and simplicity of California cuisine. If you've never tried raw artichokes and fennel, this salad is an easy introduction. You'll be impressed with the way this simple treatment adds sophistication, flavor, and texture to the dish. Save some of the feathery fennel fronds to finish and garnish the salad. You should make the salad right before you are ready to eat, but once the vegetables are trimmed, making the salad takes only a couple of minutes, even less if you use a mandolin.

LISA: This entrée is perfect for a quick spring dinner. While I usually make it with a rib or loin chop, it is also good made with a lamb steak from the leg. It is fine to vary the nuts and herbs we suggest in the crust; use what you have on hand. If you don't have a sauté pan that can go under the broiler, simply transfer the chops to a baking dish, but I like the notion of one less thing to clean.

LEMON AND ROSEMARY CRUSTED LAMB CHOPS

2 or 3 lamb chops, cut 1-inch thick (about 9 oz total)

Salt and freshly ground pepper as needed

CRUST

¼ cup fresh white breadcrumbs

1 tbsp chopped toasted walnuts

1 tbsp chopped parsley

½ clove garlic

¼ tsp chopped rosemary

1 tsp soft butter

¼ tsp lemon zest

½ tsp lemon juice

½ tsp olive oil

Fennel and Artichoke Salad (follows)

1. Trim any excess fat from the lamb chops (there should be some fat left on the chops to keep them moist as they cook). Season them with salt and pepper. Set aside.

2. Combine the ingredients for the crust in a food processor and process until very fine. Transfer to a bowl and set aside. (The crust can be stored in the refrigerator for up to 2 days or in the freezer for up to 2 weeks.)

3. Preheat the broiler to high.

4. Heat the olive oil a small sauté pan (one with an oven-proof handle, if you have one)

over medium-high heat. Add the seasoned lamb chops. Cook until brown on both sides, 4 to 5 minutes total cooking time. (The lamb chops will be slightly undercooked at this point, but will finish cooking to medium-rare when they go under the broiler in the next step. If you prefer your lamb more well-done, cook it a minute or so longer on each side.)

5. Use a soupspoon to mound and pack the crust mixture on top of each chop. Broil the chops until the crust is golden and crisp, about 3 minutes. Serve the chops with the fennel and artichoke salad.

FENNEL AND ARTICHOKE SALAD

1 small fennel bulb, trimmed and cored

Juice of ½ lemon

1 jumbo artichoke, trimmed

2 tbsp extra-virgin olive oil

1 tbsp chopped parsley

1 tbsp chopped fennel frond

Salt and freshly ground pepper as needed

Shaved Parmesan Curls (page 140)

1. Reserve a bit of the fennel fronds for a garnish. Shave the fennel into paper-thin slices using a Japanese mandolin or a very sharp knife (you should have ¾ to 1 cup). Toss in a bowl with a bit of the lemon juice.

2. Shave the artichoke bottom into paper-thin slices using a Japanese mandolin or a very sharp knife (you should have ¾ to 1 cup). Immediately add the artichokes to the fennel, tossing with more lemon juice to prevent browning.

3. Add the olive oil, chopped parsley, chopped fennel frond, salt, and pepper. Toss to coat the vegetables evenly. Taste and add more lemon juice, if needed. Serve the salad topped with a few Parmesan curls.

italian chicken ciabatta

A TOSSED GREEN SALAD is all you need to make this satisfying sandwich into a meal. If you prefer, use a 3- or 4-inch-long piece of bread cut from a loaf of good quality, crusty French bread.

1 tsp olive oil

½ cup thinly sliced red pepper

½ cup thinly sliced onion

¾ tsp finely chopped rosemary

½ tsp crushed fennel seeds

¼ tsp crushed red pepper, or to taste

1 tsp balsamic vinegar

Salt and freshly ground pepper as needed

1 tbsp mayonnaise

½ tsp minced garlic

½ tsp lemon juice

1 small boneless skinless chicken breast (about 4 oz)

1 small ciabatta roll

3 tbsp grated Fontina cheese

1 handful baby spinach, (about ½ oz)

1. Preheat the grill to medium-high heat.
2. Heat the oil in a small skillet over medium-low heat. Add the pepper, onion, rosemary, fennel, crushed red pepper, and a pinch of salt. Cook, stirring occasionally, until the onion is golden, about 5 minutes. Add the balsamic vinegar and stir to combine. Taste, season with salt and pepper, and set aside.
3. In a small bowl, stir together the mayonnaise, garlic, and lemon juice. Season with salt and pepper. Set aside.
4. Season the chicken with salt and pepper. Grill over direct heat, turning once, until cooked through, about 10 minutes. Let the chicken rest for 5 minutes.
5. Meanwhile, slice the ciabatta roll in half and warm the inside of the roll on the grill, 1 or 2 minutes. Spread both halves with the mayonnaise mixture and sprinkle with the cheese and then the spinach. Slice the chicken, layer it on the bottom of the roll, and top with the pepper-and-onion mixture. Close the sandwich and secure with toothpicks.
6. Return the sandwich to the grill and cook a few minutes on both sides until crisped and warmed. Slice in half and serve immediately.

STRAWBERRY RHUBARB FOOL

WELCOME SPRING TO the table with this classic dessert. Fools, once popular in England as well as New England, deserve to be brought back to our culinary repertoire.

While the British fool often features gooseberries, other fruits can be cooked and puréed to make a fool, such as berries, plums, peaches, and apricots. This is a good way to use up fruits that are very ripe and need to be eaten. The purée can be prepared several days ahead and refrigerated until needed. Bring it to room temperature before folding in the cream. If you find that the fruit is still too stiff, add a drop or two of orange juice to lighten it before you fold it into the whipped cream.

1 rhubarb stalk (about 3 oz)

¼ vanilla bean

4 tsp sugar

4 strawberries, stemmed and sliced

3 tbsp heavy cream

A few toasted almonds, chopped

1. Cut the rhubarb in half lengthwise and then crosswise into ½-inch pieces. Put the pieces in small microwaveable bowl with a ¼ teaspoon of water. Split the vanilla bean open with the tip of a paring knife and scrape out the seeds. Add the vanilla pod and the seeds along with the sugar to the rhubarb.

2. Microwave on high for 3 minutes. Stir to heat the rhubarb evenly and microwave on high for 1 minute. Add the strawberries and microwave for 1 minute. Stir and then finish microwaving, another 1 minute. The fruit should be very hot and tender.

3. Remove the vanilla pod from the fruit mixture, then mash the fruit with the back of a table fork until completely puréed. You should have 4 to 5 tablespoons of fruit purée. Set the purée aside to cool to room temperature.

4. Whip the heavy cream to soft peaks. Fold the rhubarb-strawberry mixture into the cream with a spatula. (If you fold it in just part-way, you'll have attractive swirls and streaks of fruit and cream.) Spoon into a serving bowl and sprinkle with a few chopped toasted almonds.

apricot pudding soufflé

THIS SOUFFLÉ HAS a delicious sweet, tart flavor and a beautiful color. We often vary the ingredients depending upon our pantry or our mood. For instance, try pistachios instead of almonds, orange peel instead of lemon, or add a drop of orange flower water to the apricots when you purée them.

MAKES 2 PUDDINGS

1 tbsp toasted almonds

3 tbsp granulated sugar, divided use

2 tsp melted butter as needed for coating soufflé molds

¼ cup chopped dried apricots

¼ cup dry white wine

1 strip lemon peel (about ½ inch square)

1 egg, separated

3 tbsp cream cheese

Pinch of salt

Pinch of cream of tartar

Whipped cream, crème fraîche, or ice cream (optional)

1. Combine the almonds with 1 tablespoon of sugar in a small food processor, and pulse until the nuts are finely ground. Coat the inside of two 6-oz soufflé cups with the melted butter. Divide the sugar-and-almond mixture between the cups and swirl to completely coat bottoms and sides. Pour out any of the mixture that isn't clinging to the mold into a small dish and set aside.

2. Preheat the oven to 400°F.

3. Combine the apricots, white wine, and lemon peel in a small microwaveable dish. Cover and microwave on high until the fruit is very soft, about 2 minutes.

4. Combine the apricots, egg yolk, and cream cheese in a small food processor and process until smooth. Transfer to a bowl and set aside.

5. Whip the egg white, salt, and cream of tartar in a small bowl until soft peaks form. Gradually add the remaining 2 tablespoons of sugar while continuing to whip, until the egg white is stiff and glossy. Carefully fold one-fourth of the white into the soufflé base to lighten it, then fold in the remaining white.

6. Spoon the pudding mixture into the prepared soufflé cups. Sprinkle the tops with ½ teaspoon of the reserved almond-sugar mixture. (At this point, the soufflés are ready to bake or freeze for later use; see note below.) Bake until the pudding is puffed and just set, about 15 minutes. Serve immediately with the accompaniment of your choice.

Whipping sugar into the egg white stabilizes the soufflé, so it will hold up for several days in the freezer before you bake it. Once the soufflé is in the cup, wrap it with foil and freeze up to 5 days. Bake the unthawed soufflé, uncovered, 22 minutes at 400°F.

strawberries with chocolate grand marnier sabayon

WHEN THE SEASONS change, try this dessert with other fruits, such as pitted and lightly sautéed Bing or Queen Ann cherries with Kirsch in the spring. In the winter, blood oranges with Grand Marnier or Cointreau are a superb pairing. Two summertime combinations to try are raspberries with Framboise or peaches with Amaretto.

A sabayon cooks very quickly and, once prepared, should be served right away. Having everything ready to go is important to the success of the dish. Use a high-quality bittersweet chocolate like Valrhona for a pure chocolate flavor without too much sweetness.

¾ cup hulled and quartered strawberries

½ tsp granulated sugar

2 tsp julienned orange zest (see Note)

1 egg yolk

1 tbsp sugar

2 tbsp white wine

1 tbsp water

½ tsp Grand Marnier

2 tbsp finely grated bittersweet chocolate

1. Toss the strawberries and sugar together in a dish and spoon them into a brandy snifter or wine glass.

2. Fill the bottom of a double boiler halfway with water and bring it to boil over high heat. Add the orange zest and cook for 2 minutes. Scoop out the zest with a small strainer or slotted spoon, rinse under cold water, pat dry in a paper towel, and set aside. Reduce the heat to low and keep the pot of water at a simmer.

3. In the top of your double boiler, whisk together the yolk and sugar until light and almost white in color. Place over the simmering water (be certain that the bottom of bowl does not touch the water).

4. Add the wine and water to the yolk mixture and whisk constantly over the simmering water until sabayon doubles in volume and thickens, 3 to 5 minutes.

5. Remove the sabayon from the heat and add the Grand Marnier and chocolate. Continue to whisk until the chocolate is completely dissolved. Spoon the sabayon over the strawberries, top with the zest, and serve.

MAKING JULIENNED ZEST

There is nothing wrong with just grating some orange zest over the sabayon, but if you take a minute to cut the zest into julienne and blanch it as described in step 2 at left, the flavor and texture becomes more refined. To prepare the zest, use a vegetable peeler to cut two or three wide strips (about ¼ inch wide) from an orange. If there is any white pith left on the zest, scrape it away. Cut the strips crosswise into very thin strips.

CHAPTER TWO

Summer

NO MATTER WHAT part of the country you live in, summer is the season of abundance. Farmers' markets are full to overflowing, and backyard gardens are starting to produce in earnest. Who wouldn't want to cook with all those colors and flavors for inspiration?

VEGETABLES

Artichokes (limited availability)

Beans

Beets

Carrots

Celery

Cucumber

Eggplant

Garlic

Greens (arugula, lettuce, spinach, watercress)

Onions

Peppers

Okra

Potatoes

Summer Squash

Sweet Corn

Tomatillo

Tomatoes

Zucchini

FRUITS

Apricots

Blackberries

Blueberries

Boysenberries

Cherries

Currants

Figs

Melons

Peaches

Raspberries

Strawberries

melon and buffalo milk mozzarella salad

BUFFALO MILK MOZZARELLA has a silky consistency and delicious flavor, well worth the extra cost. However, good quality fresh cow's milk mozzarella can be substituted.

1 cantaloupe wedge (about ⅛ melon), or another variety
of ripe melon

1 oz fresh buffalo mozzarella, sliced

1½ tsp mint leaves, cut into thin ribbons

1½ tsp basil leaves, cut into thin ribbons

⅛ tsp grated lemon zest

Freshly cracked white or black pepper

Salt

Extra-virgin olive oil for drizzling

Cut the melon away from the rind and slice the melon thin. Fan the melon slices around the outside of the plate and the mozzarella slices in the center. Sprinkle with the mint, basil, lemon zest, pepper and a pinch of salt. Drizzle with olive oil. Serve immediately.

mediterranean rice salad with spinach

LISA: This salad can easily become an entrée with the addition of a few cubes of feta and slices of tomato and cucumber on the side. If I've planned a dinner with rice earlier in the week, I make a little extra and enjoy this salad a few nights later.

¾ cup cooked rice, preferably basmati

1 small scallion with 2 inches green top, thinly sliced

1 tbsp currants

1½ tsp extra-virgin olive oil, divided use

2 cups coarsely chopped fresh spinach leaves (about 2 oz)

1½ tsp lemon juice

¼ tsp lemon zest

Salt and freshly ground pepper as needed

1 tsp toasted pine nuts

1. Combine the rice, scallion, and currants in a bowl. Set aside.

2. Heat ½ teaspoon olive oil in a small sauté pan over medium-high heat. Add the spinach and cook, stirring until just wilted, 2 to 3 minutes. Remove with a slotted spoon, lightly squeezing out excess moisture. Add the drained spinach to the rice.

3. Whisk the remaining teaspoon of olive oil together with the lemon juice and zest. Season with salt and pepper to taste, then pour over the rice-spinach mixture. Toss to coat evenly and adjust seasoning if needed.

4. Sprinkle the salad with the toasted pine nuts. Serve at once.

taco salad

LISA: This salad features everything I love about Mexican food and, by being careful with the ingredients I choose and their quantities, I can enjoy it without the guilt that usually follows a calorie-laden meal. You can use purchased salsa, but our recipe below takes just a few minutes to put together and has an unbeatable fresh taste.

MARK: Taco salad might seem like a cliché to many people, but I urge you to try this fresh tasting version. The recipe lends itself well to a number of substitutions that are still fresh-tasting and healthy. For instance, it's a great way to enjoy fresh corn, but frozen corn works well, too. Replace the black beans with pinto or kidney beans. Add diced zucchini to the filling if you have some available. If fresh tomatoes are in season, use them instead of canned.

TACO SALAD

MEAT FILLING

½ tsp canola oil

¼ cup diced onion

1 tsp chopped garlic

2 oz ground buffalo or turkey

1 tsp chili powder

½ tsp ground cumin

⅛ tsp dried oregano

Pinch chipotle chili pepper flakes

⅓ cup diced canned tomatoes

¼ cup cooked black beans (page 136)

¼ cup corn kernels (fresh or frozen and thawed)

¼ cup Homemade Chicken Stock (page 134)

1 tbsp sour cream (preferably lowfat)

Salt and freshly ground pepper as needed

SALAD

4 cups shredded lettuce

1 tbsp sour cream (preferably lowfat)

2 tbsp shredded cheddar

Salsa (recipe follows)

Baked tortilla chips

1. Heat the oil in a medium sauté pan over medium heat. Add the onion and garlic. Sauté, stirring frequently, until softened, about 1 minute.

2. Crumble the ground meat into the pan and cook, stirring occasionally to break up the meat, until browned, about 4 minutes. Add the chili powder, cumin, oregano, and chipotle flakes, and cook another minute, stirring to blend the spices into the meat.

3. Add the tomatoes, beans, corn, and stock. Bring to a simmer and cook over low heat until flavorful and very hot, about 5 minutes. Remove the pan from the heat and stir in the sour cream. Season with salt and pepper. This filling can be made a day or two ahead and stored in a covered container in the refrigerator for up to 2 days. Reheat it gently in a pan over low heat or in the microwave.

4. To assemble the salad, mound the lettuce on a dinner or soup plate. Top with the meat mixture, sour cream, cheese, and salsa. Serve with baked tortilla chips on the side.

SALSA

⅓ cup halved cherry tomatoes

1 scallion, chopped

2 tbsp diced red pepper

1½ tsp chopped cilantro

1 tsp chopped jalapeño, or to taste

1 tsp fresh lime juice

Salt and freshly ground pepper as needed

Combine all the salsa ingredients together in a small bowl. Season to taste with salt and pepper.

PAN BAGNA

LISA: Try this Mediterranean sandwich in the summer when vegetables are at their peak. We have listed ingredients for a fairly traditional combination, but leave it up to you to layer the sandwich as you like, choosing your own seasonal favorites.

MARK: Three things are a must for pan bagna: good crusty bread, juicy, garden-ripe tomatoes, and a generous dose of fruity extra-virgin olive oil. After the sandwich is assembled, tradition has it that the sandwich should rest for 30 minutes to allow the tomato juices and olive oil to soften the bread and meld the flavors together.

French baguette or French roll

1 garlic clove, crushed

Extra-virgin olive oil as needed

Sliced ripe beefsteak tomato

Salt and freshly ground pepper as needed

Hard-boiled egg, sliced

Cucumber, peeled and sliced thin

Red or green bell pepper, seeded and sliced thin

Pitted black olives (Niçoise, if available)

Anchovies or canned tuna, optional

1. Split the baguette or roll and pull out some of the soft interior of the bread. Rub the inside of the bread with the garlic clove and then discard the garlic.

2. Drizzle the bread with the olive oil. Add the tomato slices and season with salt and pepper. Continue layering the sandwich with the remaining ingredients, adding anchovies or tuna if desired. Close the sandwich and let it rest for 30 minutes before serving.

gazpacho with shrimp

LISA: We like the combination of the cool soup with the slightly warm shrimp, but if you are in a hurry, you can always use purchased cooked shrimp. Serve this refreshing soup with French bread slices that have been brushed with olive oil and toasted.

MARK: Although the soup needs to chill after being made, this can still be a quick dinner. Purée the soup, pour it into a bowl, and then chill it quickly by putting it in the freezer or over an ice bath. Stir the soup occasionally while cutting the vegetable garnishes and poaching the shrimp. When the soup is cold, the freshly poached shrimp makes a nice temperature contrast.

1 slice baguette (about ½ oz), cubed

¼ cup cold water

1½ cups coarsely chopped tomato (about 9 oz), plus 1 tbsp small-dice for garnish

2 tbsp coarsely chopped red onion, plus 1 tbsp small-dice for garnish

1 cup coarsely chopped cucumber, plus 1 tbsp small-dice for garnish

½ cup coarsely chopped bell peppers (mix of colors), plus 1 tbsp small-dice for garnish

½ tsp minced garlic

1 tbsp red wine or sherry vinegar

2 tbsp extra-virgin olive oil, plus additional for serving

Salt and freshly ground black pepper as needed

5 large shrimp, peeled and poached (see Note)

2 leaves basil, cut into chiffonade

1. Soak the baguette in the cold water until the bread absorbs the water, about 5 minutes.

2. Transfer the soaked bread to a blender; add the tomato, onion, cucumber, peppers, garlic, vinegar, and olive oil. Purée the gazpacho in a blender until it is relatively smooth, but with just a little bit of texture. Season with salt, pepper, and more vinegar, if necessary. Refrigerate until it is chilled.

3. Ladle the gazpacho into a large soup plate. Arrange the shrimp in the center in a spiral and sprinkle with a garnish of neatly diced vegetables and basil. Drizzle the soup with a few drops of olive oil, and serve.

POACHING SHRIMP

Peel and devein 5 large shrimp. In a small sauté pan, combine 1 cup water with a bay leaf, 5 peppercorns, 5 coriander seeds (optional), and 1 parsley sprig. Bring the water to a boil, then simmer for 2 minutes to flavor the water. Add the shrimp, turn off the heat, cover the pan tightly, and let sit, turning once, until the shrimp are cooked through, 2 to 4 minutes. Remove them from the water and let them drain before adding to the soup.

TOPPING AND BAKING PIZZAS

LISA: Pizza is so versatile. You can change the toppings to suit the season and your taste. By the end of the summer, my garden is overflowing with vegetables. They make standout pizza toppings with just a bit of shredded fresh basil or a spoonful of pungent pesto and a few slices of fresh mozzarella.

The three main points to remember for vegetable toppings are these:

- *The toppings should be moist, but not wet, when you add them.*

- *The toppings should never overcrowd the surface of the pizza.*

- *The toppings should be fully cooked by the time the crust is golden.*

Here are a few tricks for getting your toppings ready:

EGGPLANT: Leave the skin on the eggplant if it is tender; peel it away if it is too tough to pierce easily with your thumbnail. To avoid leftovers, I look for the long, thin Asian eggplants, which are much smaller than the globe variety. Broiling the eggplant before you put it on your pizza assures that it has a full flavor and is tender enough to bite into easily.

ZUCCHINI: Broil zucchini to give it a jump start on cooking, as well as to add flavor and color.

ONIONS AND PEPPERS: No need to precook. Just slice thin and scatter on top. For a more robust flavor, they can be marinated in a bit of vinaigrette and drained well before adding as a topping.

TOMATOES: Fresh tomatoes add a lighter dimension to vegetable pizza, rather than the usual tomato sauce. Because of their high natural moisture content, tomatoes need to be dried a little. Put the tomato slices between a few layers of paper towels to drain for 15 minutes or so. Press gently to blot up any extra moisture right before you add them to your pizza. If you are using cherry tomatoes, cut them in half and put them on the pizza with the cut side facing up. Oven-dried Tomatoes (page 141) or slivered sun-dried tomatoes also are great options to get tomato flavor without making your pizza topping soggy.

FRESH MOZZARELLA: There is a world of difference in both flavor and texture between fresh mozzarella and the type that is often sold already shredded for pizza. Fresh mozzarella is very moist and doesn't shred easily, so you should slice it thin. Slicing the mozzarella releases some of the moisture, so, depending on the variety, you might need to gently press the slices between a few layers of paper towels to blot up the liquid, as described above for blotting tomatoes. It is added at the end of the pizza cooking time to retain its delicate texture and creaminess.

eggplant, zucchini, and oven-dried tomato pizza

LISA: The topping for this pizza is a good way to enjoy healthy fresh vegetables. I vary the ingredients according to what I have available, sometimes using a fresh sliced plum tomato instead of oven-dried or yellow squash instead of zucchini.

MARK: I make a more robust variation of this pizza substituting raw onion slices for the zucchini. After taking the pizza out of the oven, I scatter some olives and torn proscuitto over it.

4 or 5 slices eggplant, cut ⅓ inch thick

4 or 5 slices zucchini, cut on a diagonal ⅓ inch thick

Extra-virgin olive oil as needed

Salt and freshly ground pepper as needed

Cornmeal for dusting

Flour for rolling dough

One 6-oz ball Pizza Dough (page 142)

1 tsp minced garlic

8 Oven-dried Tomatoes (page 141)

2 to 3 oz fresh mozzarella, sliced thin and blotted dry, if necessary

2 or 3 basil leaves, torn into pieces

1. Preheat the broiler.

2. Put the eggplant and zucchini slices on a nonstick baking sheet. Brush the tops with olive oil. Season with salt and pepper. Broil on the first side until well-browned. Turn the slices, brush with a little more oil, and season lightly with salt and pepper. Broil on the second side until browned. Remove to a plate or platter and set aside.

3. Place a pizza stone on the bottom rack in the oven. Dust a pizza peel (or a baking sheet with no sides) with cornmeal and set aside. Preheat the oven to 500°F, allowing 30 minutes for the pizza stone to heat thoroughly.

4. Flour your work surface lightly, and then roll or stretch the dough into an 8-inch circle. Transfer the dough to the prepared peel or baking sheet. Brush the dough with a little olive oil, and sprinkle with garlic. Arrange the eggplant, zucchini, and tomatoes over the dough, leaving a ¾-inch border. Be careful not to overcrowd the surface.

5. Slide the pizza from the peel or baking sheet onto the pizza stone. Bake until the crust is browned, about 10 minutes. Lay the mozzarella slices on top and continue to bake until the cheese is melted, 1 or 2 minutes more.

6. Scatter the basil leaves over the pizza, cut into slices, and serve hot.

tomato, mozzarella, prosciutto, and arugula pizza

LISA: The pizza toppings here leave plenty of room for variation. If you don't have pesto, sprinkle some chopped fresh herbs—basil, parsley, oregano, marjoram—on top of the prosciutto. Top this pizza with any tasty greens you like, perhaps some baby spinach or watercress.

MARK: Sometimes I make this pizza with pancetta in place of the prosciutto. I add it to the pizza at the same time as the tomatoes and onions. As the pizza bakes, the pancetta adds a layer of rich flavor.

Cornmeal for dusting

Flour for rolling dough

One 6-oz ball Pizza Dough (page 142)

1½ tsp extra-virgin olive oil

1 garlic clove, finely minced

9 small cherry tomatoes, halved

¼ cup thinly sliced onion

1 tbsp Pesto (page 140)

Salt and freshly ground pepper as needed

2 to 3 oz fresh mozzarella, sliced thin and blotted dry, if necessary

½ cup arugula leaves

1 slice prosciutto, torn into large pieces

1. Place a pizza stone on the bottom rack in the oven. Dust a pizza peel (or a baking sheet with no sides) with cornmeal and set aside. Preheat the oven to 500°F, allowing at least 30 minutes for the pizza stone to heat thoroughly.

2. Flour your work surface lightly and roll or stretch the dough into an 8-inch circle. Transfer the dough to the prepared peel or baking sheet.

3. Mix the olive oil and garlic together in a small dish. Brush evenly over the pizza dough. Scatter the tomatoes, cut side up, and the onions evenly over the pizza, being careful not to overcrowd the surface. Drop small spoonfuls of pesto over the pizza. Season with salt and pepper.

4. Slide the pizza from the peel or baking sheet onto the pizza stone. Bake until done, about 10 minutes. Lay the mozzarella slices on top and continue to bake until cheese is melted and lightly browned, 1 or 2 minutes more.

5. Remove the pizza from the oven, top with arugula and prosciutto. Cut into slices and serve.

asian eggplant

MARK: Eggplant is a vegetable that is too often overlooked. In this version, its delicate texture comes to life when paired with the spicy, *umami* (meaty) flavors of the sauce. Asian chefs truly understand how to layer textures and flavors, demonstrated here by the final addition of peanuts and cilantro that serves as much more than a garnish.

LISA: Serve this vegetable as the backdrop to a piece of simply grilled fish or pork and you have a fabulous meal.

SAUCE

1½ tsp fish sauce

1 tsp lime juice

1 tsp water

¼ tsp soy sauce

½ lb Asian eggplant, sliced ½ inch thick

Salt and freshly ground pepper as needed

2 tsp peanut oil plus as needed for brushing

½ clove garlic, minced

½ tsp chopped fresh ginger

1 tsp finely chopped serrano chile, including seeds

2 scallions, including 3 inches of green, sliced thin on a diagonal

GARNISH

Chopped toasted peanuts

Whole cilantro leaves

1. Mix together the sauce ingredients in a small bowl and set aside.

2. Preheat a grill to medium heat.

3. Season the eggplant slices with salt and pepper. Brush them on both sides lightly with enough oil to coat.

4. Grill the eggplant until lightly browned on the both sides, turning once, about 6 minutes total. Remove to a platter.

5. Heat 2 teaspoons peanut oil in a small skillet over medium heat. Add the garlic and ginger and sauté, stirring constantly, until fragrant, about 15 seconds. Add the chile and scallions and sauté about 10 seconds. Add the sauce and stir to combine. Pour the sauce over the eggplant. Finish the dish by sprinkling the peanuts and cilantro over the top. Serve warm or at room temperature.

CEDAR PLANKED SALMON WITH HIS-AND-HERS SEASONAL CORN SAUTÉ

MARK: Native American Indians in the Pacific Northwest used to barbecue salmon splayed on planks of aromatic cedar propped near an open fire. King salmon, available in the later part of summer, is lean, full flavored, and holds up nicely to the smoky cedar. Use untreated cedar planks meant for cooking. Our recipe calls for cooking the salmon in the oven, but it can also be cooked on an outdoor grill with a cover. Let the plank heat up over the coals until the bottom starts to smoke before adding the salmon. In either case, we like to take the extra step of broiling the fish for a minute at the end to add color.

LISA: Not surprisingly, we couldn't agree on which corn dish went better with the salmon. We even asked another couple to help settle the debate, and, once again, there was a gender-specific preference. So to keep the peace, we offer both. Mark's is a heartier dish with potatoes served hot from the pan and highlights the salmon's smoky cedar flavor. My version is more like a salad and includes cucumbers and zucchini to tone down the smoke and refresh the palate.

CEDAR-PLANKED SALMON

1 piece salmon fillet (about 5 oz)

Salt and freshly ground black pepper as needed

1 tbsp maple syrup

1 tsp lemon juice

½ tsp soy sauce

½ tsp whole-grain mustard

½ tsp grated ginger

1. Place a small cedar plank on the middle rack of the oven and then preheat the oven to 350 F until the plank becomes fragrant, about 30 minutes. Season the salmon with salt and pepper; set aside.

2. Combine the maple syrup, lemon juice, soy sauce, mustard, and ginger in small dish. Microwave on high until reduced to a light glaze, about 45 seconds. Brush the salmon with the glaze and place it directly on the hot cedar plank. Bake the salmon until it is just opaque in the center, 15 to 20 minutes.

3. Turn the broiler on high and broil the salmon until it is lightly browned, about 1 minute. Serve the salmon with one of the corn sautés.

HIS CORN SAUTÉ

2 tiny new potatoes (1 oz)

10 to 12 haricots verts or small green beans (1 oz), trimmed and cut into 1-inch pieces

2 tsp extra-virgin olive oil

2 tbsp finely chopped shallots

2 to 3 chanterelle mushrooms (1 oz), wiped clean and sliced

1 tsp minced garlic

1 tsp finely chopped rosemary

1 ear sweet corn, kernels cut from the cob

⅓ cup diced tomato, peeled and seeded

1. Cook the potatoes in a small pot of simmering, lightly salted water until tender when pierced with the tip of a knife, 8 to 10 minutes. Remove the potatoes with a slotted spoon and cut them into quarters; reserve.

2. Bring the water back to a boil, add the green beans, and cook until bright green and just tender, about 3 minutes. Drain the beans, plunge them into in a bowl of ice water, and then let them drain; pat dry on a paper towel.

3. Heat the oil in a small sauté pan over medium heat. Add the shallots and sauté, stirring constantly, until translucent, about 1 minute. Add the mushrooms, garlic, and rosemary and sauté, stirring occasionally, until the mushrooms start to brown and are tender, about 5 minutes. Add the corn and cook 2 minutes. Add the potatoes, green beans, and tomato. Stir or toss until blended and all of the ingredients are heated through, about 2 minutes. Season with salt and pepper.

HER CORN SAUTÉ

3 tsp extra-virgin olive oil, divided use

1 ear sweet corn, kernels cut from cob

½ cup sliced zucchini, quartered lengthwise
before slicing (2 oz)

¼ cup small-dice cucumber

¼ cup small-dice tomato

4 basil leaves, chopped

2 tsp lemon juice

2 tsp extra-virgin olive oil

Salt and freshly ground pepper

Heat 1 teaspoon of olive oil in a small sauté pan over medium-high heat. Add the corn and zucchini and cook, stirring occasionally, until just barely cooked, about 1 minute. Spoon into a bowl, add the remaining the ingredients, and mix well. Season to taste with salt and pepper.

ratatouille and polenta

LISA: The inspiration for this dish came from a trip many years ago to the renowned Chez Panisse Café in Berkeley, California. While waiting for our food, we watched the table next to us being served a platter of warm, creamy polenta paired with a fragrant ratatouille. Today, it is a dish I turn to often to enjoy the pleasures of seasonal and rustic cooking—comfort food at it's best. The ratatouille an be made several days in advance, and actually improves in flavor as it sits.

MARK: The quantities listed here for the vegetables do not need to be exact, by any means, and should be varied according to what you have and like. Double the ratatouille recipe to have some ready for the Ratatouille Tartlet (page 46) or to serve as a side dish with grilled or roasted lamb or chicken.

RATATOUILLE

TRADITIONALLY, THE VEGETABLES for ratatouille are sautéed separately in olive oil. We have chosen to oven roast them all together, which imparts deeper flavors, uses a lot less oil, and is much easier, too.

2 cups large-dice eggplant (about 6 oz)

½ medium large-dice zucchini (about 3 oz)

½ medium large-dice yellow squash (about 3 oz)

⅓ red pepper, cut into large dice

¼ onion, cut into large dice

1½ tbsp extra-virgin olive oil

Salt and freshly ground black pepper as needed

½ cup halved cherry tomatoes or ⅓ cup chopped, seeded tomato

1 garlic clove, chopped

2 tbsp red wine

¼ cup Homemade Chicken Stock (page 134)

2 tbsp slivered basil

1. Preheat the oven to 425°F.

2. Place the eggplant, zucchini, squash, red pepper, and onion on a baking sheet. Drizzle the olive oil over the vegetables, season with salt and pepper, and toss until they are evenly coated. Bake, uncovered, for 20 minutes. Add the tomatoes and garlic, and turn with a spatula to distribute them evenly. Bake until all of the vegetables are tender, another 10 minutes.

3. Remove the pan from the oven. Add the wine and stock; mix well, scraping the bottom of the pan to release any browned bits. Pour the ratatouille into a small casserole dish along with the wine and stock. Return to the oven and bake, uncovered, until the vegetables are tender and the wine has mellowed and cooked down a little, another 10 minutes; there should still be some liquid in the dish.

4. Season the ratatouille with salt and pepper and sprinkle with the basil. Serve on top of the polenta in a heated soup plate.

POLENTA

IF YOU ARE hesitating because you don't want to spend time stirring polenta as it cooks, this recipe may change your mind. The polenta is cooked in the oven with little stirring required. Opt for stone-ground cornmeal for the best texture and richest flavor.

¼ cup medium coarse or coarse stone-ground cornmeal

1 cup water

¼ tsp salt

¼ cup milk

½ tsp butter, optional

1 tbsp grated Parmesan

Salt and freshly ground black pepper as needed

1. Preheat the oven to 350°F.
2. Whisk together the cornmeal, water, and salt. Pour into a heavy 1-quart casserole dish. Bake, uncovered, for 40 minutes; the polenta will be nearly done at this point.
3. Add the milk and the butter, if using, and stir well until the butter is blended in and the polenta is smooth. Continue to bake until the polenta is fully cooked and creamy, 10 minutes more. Stir in the Parmesan, and season with salt and pepper to taste.

RATATOUILLE TARTLET

THIS DELICIOUS TARTLET takes just a few minutes to put together, but it has all the complex flavors of a slow-cooked meal.

Flour for rolling dough

2½ oz Pâte Brisée (page 143)

1 cup Ratatouille (page 44)

1 tbsp sliced pitted black olives, preferably Kalamata or Niçoise

1½ tbsp finely grated Parmesan, divided use

1½ tbsp grated Fontina, divided use

1. Preheat the oven to 400°F.
2. On a lightly floured surface, roll the pâte brisée into a 6½-inch square, about ⅛-inch-thick, and place the dough on a baking sheet lined with parchment.
3. If the ratatouille is very saucy, lightly drain off the excess liquid with a slotted spoon. Mix the ratatouille in a small bowl with the olives and half of the cheeses. Pile the mixture in the center of the dough, leaving a ¾- to 1-inch border around the edge.
4. Fold the dough up over the edges of the ratatouille, pinching it at intervals to keep it in place. Sprinkle the remaining cheeses on top. Bake until the dough is golden brown and crisp, about 30 minutes.

grilled tuna with pesto and tomato salad

LISA: The key to the success of this dish is using ingredients that are impeccably fresh and at their seasonal peak. A perfect summer tomato needs very little embellishment, just a touch of vinegar and olive oil.

MARK: When I am in an apartment during the week, I cannot have a grill so I use a grill pan on the stove. Granted, it does not have the flavor of charcoal, but it does a good job of searing food.

Oil for brushing grill as needed

1 fresh tuna steak (about 5 oz)

1½ tsp extra-virgin olive oil, plus additional for brushing tuna

Salt and freshly ground pepper as needed

½ cup medium-dice tomatoes

1½ tsp balsamic vinegar

Salt and freshly ground pepper as needed

Seasonal vegetables: a combination of eggplant, yellow
    squash, zucchini, and red pepper (about 6 oz total)

Pesto (page 140)

1. Preheat the grill to high heat. Brush the grates carefully with oil. Brush the tuna lightly with olive oil and season with a pinch of salt and pepper. Set aside.

2. Combine the tomatoes, vinegar, and olive oil in a bowl. Add salt and pepper to taste and set aside. (The excess dressing on the tomatoes becomes a basting liquid for the grilled vegetables.)

3. Prepare the vegetables for the grill: Depending on their sizes and shapes, slice the eggplant, zucchini, and yellow squash ½-inch-thick; halve, quarter, or leave them whole if small, such as baby squash. Seed and quarter the pepper.

4. Brush the vegetables lightly with the dressing that the tomatoes are marinating in. Grill them over the outer edge of the heat until they are browned on both sides and fully cooked, about 8 minutes total.

5. After turning the vegetables once, add the tuna to the grill, placing it over direct heat. Grill on the first side until the tuna is golden, about 3 minutes. Turn once and finish cooking to the doneness you like, another 2 to 3 minutes for medium-rare or a minute longer if you prefer your tuna medium to medium-well.

6. Serve the tuna on a plate with the grilled vegetables. Spoon the tomatoes and their remaining dressing over the tuna and top with a dollop of pesto.

The grilled vegetables can be varied according to the season or what you have on hand. As summer ends and fall approaches, radicchio, mushrooms, and endive would be good. Asparagus is great cooked on the grill in the early summer, as are scallions.

pasta with swordfish, marinated tomatoes, and salsa verde

MARK: Other meaty fish, such as tuna or mahi-mahi, can be used instead of the swordfish in this dish. The fish just needs to be thick enough to be skewered and firm enough to hold its shape while grilling on a skewer. The fish can also be pan sautéed in olive oil until the bread-crumbs are a light brown and the fish is cooked through.

LISA: Salsa Verde is quick to put together when you are making a small amount. However, purchased tapenade or salsa verde can be substituted.

PASTA WITH SWORDFISH AND MARINATED TOMATOES

MARINATED TOMATOES

1 cup diced tomatoes

1 tbsp finely chopped shallots

½ tsp balsamic vinegar

Salt and freshly ground pepper as needed

SWORDFISH

4 oz swordfish, cut into 1½-inch cubes

Salt and ground black pepper as needed

1 tbsp extra-virgin olive oil, or as needed for coating

2 tbsp plain dried bread crumbs

1 to 2 oz spaghetti

Salsa Verde (recipe follows) or prepared tapenade

1. Combine the tomatoes, shallots, and vinegar in a small bowl. Season with salt and pepper, and set aside to marinate while you prepare the swordfish.

2. Preheat a grill to medium-high.

3. Season the swordfish with salt and pepper. Lightly toss the fish with a small amount of olive oil, then dredge in the bread crumbs. Place the swordfish on skewers.

4. Bring a large pot of salted water to a boil. Add the spaghetti and cook according to package directions.

5. While cooking the pasta, grill the swordfish over indirect heat until slightly browned and cooked through, about 1 to 2 minutes on each side.

6. Drain the pasta, place on a plate, and top with the marinated tomatoes. Place the swordfish in a circle on top of the tomatoes, and spoon the salsa verde around the fish.

Fish is a great source of protein. Health and nutrition experts recommend that we eat it two to three times a week. However, due to concerns about the availability and safety of some varieties, it is important to be an educated consumer. We often refer to the Monterey Bay Aquarium's Seafood Watch pocket guides. The most up-to-date version is available through their website, montereybayaquarium.org.

SALSA VERDE

1 tbsp extra-virgin olive oil

1 tbsp chopped parsley

1 tbsp chopped basil

1 tbsp chopped green olives

1 tsp capers, rinsed and chopped

1 tsp minced garlic

1 anchovy filet, chopped fine

1 tbsp lemon juice

¼ tsp lemon zest

⅛ tsp cracked red pepper

Salt and freshly ground pepper as needed

Combine all of the ingredients and let the salsa marinate for at least 10 minutes. If made in advance, cover the bowl and refrigerate. The salsa will keep for up to 2 days.

SALMON WITH GINGER, BLACK PEPPER, AND ASIAN VEGETABLE STIR FRY

MARK: This is a beautiful dish with lots of color from the vegetables and a nice spiciness from the peppercorns, ginger, and jalapeño. It can be made with many different types of fish as long as the variety you choose can hold up to the spice in the ginger and pepper. Tuna, swordfish, or sea bass would be good substitutes. If you purchase more fish than you need, by all means cook it with the ginger and peppercorns. This slow-cook method produces a very moist fish that would be excellent in a salad the next day.

LISA: Much of the prep work involved in this dish could be done a day or two ahead. Clean the vegetables, but save the chopping and jalapeño for the last minute. Rice left from a previous night or quick-cooking brown rice will make putting the

dish together much faster. The peppercorns can be cracked well in advance.

1 piece salmon fillet (about 4½ to 5 oz)

Sesame oil as needed

Soy sauce as needed

½ tsp finely chopped fresh ginger

½ tsp cracked black peppercorns

SAUCE

2 tbsp chicken stock

2 tsp fish sauce

¼ tsp cornstarch

½ tsp brown sugar

½ tsp soy sauce

1½ tsp vegetable or stir fry oil

1 garlic clove, finely minced

1 whole Thai bird chile or ½ jalapeño, seeded and finely diced

9 snow peas (1 oz), stringed and cut in half on a diagonal

1 oz baby bok choy, halved or cut into 2-inch lengths if large

¼ cup thinly sliced red pepper, cut in 1-inch lengths

2 scallions with 3 inches green tops, sliced thin on diagonal

Steamed rice (page 136)

⅛ cup loosely packed cilantro leaves

1. Preheat the oven to 250°F.

2. Place the salmon in a lightly oiled individual gratin or shallow baking dish. Lightly brush salmon with a thin coat of sesame oil and soy sauce. Sprinkle with ginger and peppercorns. Bake for 30 minutes.

3. Combine the sauce ingredients, stirring well. Set aside.

4. Prepare the vegetables and have them ready next to the stove.

5. When salmon is done, remove it from oven and set aside to keep warm.

6. Heat the oil in a medium sauté pan over high heat. When the oil is hot, add the garlic and jalapeño and sauté a few seconds. Add the snow peas, bok choy, and red pepper. Sauté briefly, about 30 to 45 seconds. Stir the sauce ingredients together, add them to the pan, and bring to a boil, stirring constantly. Remove the pan from the heat and stir in the scallions.

7. Place a serving of cooked rice in middle of plate. Spoon the vegetables around the rice. Place the salmon in the center of the plate on top of the rice. Sprinkle with the cilantro and serve.

Freshly cracked black pepper adds a nice bite to this dish. It can be purchased in the spice section of a market, but it has a lot more flavor if you crack it yourself, which is easy to do. Place a small amount in a baking pan with sides. Using a heavy bottomed pot, keep part of the pot resting on the bottom of the pan and rock the handle end up and down, smashing the peppercorns until they are all coarsely chopped. Leftover pepper can be kept in a small dish by the stove for use in most cooking.

cornish hen with chutney glaze, mango and curry salad

MARK: This salad is good any time of year. Grill the hen for a different flavor and texture or pan roast it as we do here. Chicken or lamb can be substituted for the Cornish hen. Cooking times will vary.

Fresh peaches, plums or apricots can be substituted for the mango. This recipe calls for cooking an entire hen, which is probably more than you will want for dinner. Use the leftovers another day or, alternatively, you can split the hen before you roast it and freeze half to cook another time.

LISA: To make this a simple dish to put together, use our mise en place strategies: After grocery shopping, wash lettuces, spin dry, and store in plastic bags so they are ready to use when needed. The salad dressing can be made several days in advance. Some stores sell coconut and nuts already toasted, which saves you a step and valuable time.

GLAZE

1 tbsp Major Grey's chutney

1 tsp lime juice

¾ tsp canola oil, divided use

Salt and freshly ground pepper as needed

1 Cornish hen

MANGO SALAD

4 cups lettuce, such as Boston, Bibb, or green or red leaf

¼ red pepper, thinly sliced

⅓ cup medium-dice mango

2 tbsp thinly sliced red onion

1 tbsp raisins, dried cranberries, or dried cherries

SALAD DRESSING

¼ tsp curry powder

1 tsp red wine vinegar

½ tsp lime juice

2 tbsp canola oil

¼ tsp Major Grey's chutney

Salt and freshly ground pepper as needed

1 tbsp toasted slivered almonds or cashews

1 tsp toasted coconut, optional

Warmed pita bread

1. Preheat the oven to 450°F.

2. Make the chutney glaze: In a small bowl, combine the chutney, lime juice, ¼ teaspoon canola oil, salt, and pepper. Set aside.

3. With a knife or scissors, cut along both sides of the backbone to remove it from the Cornish hen, place it skin side up, and press the keel bone with the heel of your palm to even the thickness. Season on both sides with salt and pepper.

4. Heat the remaining canola oil in a medium sauté pan over medium heat. Cook the Cornish hen skin-side-down until well browned, about 10 minutes. Turn the hen,

brush with the chutney glaze, and move the pan to the oven to bake until it is cooked through, about 10 more minutes. The juices should run clear when the thigh is pierced with a small knife. Set aside and keep warm.

5. Combine all of the salad ingredients in a salad bowl. Set aside. Make the dressing: Heat the curry powder in a small nonstick skillet over low heat until the curry is toasted and fragrant. Remove to a small bowl and whisk in the remaining ingredients, seasoning with salt and pepper to taste.

6. Place the pan used for roasting the hen over low heat, stirring to release drippings. Remove the pan from the heat and whisk in the salad dressing. Toss the salad with the dressing and place on a dinner plate. Cut the hen in half and reserve half for another day. Cut the remaining half between the bones into 2 or 3 pieces and set on top of salad. Sprinkle with nuts and coconut, if using. Serve with warm pita bread.

tandoori chicken with indian-style eggplant stew

LISA: Indian food is all about creating layers of flavors through a combination of spices and cooking methods. If you do not have all of the spices listed below, give it a try anyway—you will still enjoy the dish, and might even find yourself seeking out the missing spices before your next go-round. You will be able to find most of the spices in a typical grocery store. The chicken can and should be marinated well in advance to give the yogurt marinade a chance to infuse the chicken with the spice and make the meat moist and tender.

MARK: Tandoori chicken is traditionally served with a simple platter of raw vegetables, however we've added an extra dimension here—the rich, smoky flavor of an eggplant stew.

TANDOORI CHICKEN

1 portion bone-in chicken breast (6 oz)

TANDOORI MARINADE

3 tbsp plain yogurt

2 tsp lemon juice

1 tsp grated ginger

½ tsp finely chopped garlic

⅛ tsp cayenne pepper

⅛ tsp salt

⅛ tsp ground cumin

⅛ tsp turmeric

¼ tsp ground coriander

Pinch saffron, optional

1. Use the tip of a paring knife to make 3 diagonal slits, ½-inch deep, into the chicken breast through the thickest part; set aside.

2. Combine the ingredients for the marinade in a zip-close plastic bag. Add the chicken and massage the marinade into the meat. Squeeze the air out from the bag, seal tightly, and let the chicken marinate in the refrigerator at least 8 and up to 24 hours.

3. Preheat a grill to medium-high, and lightly oil the grill rods. Remove the chicken from the marinade, scraping away any excess. Grill the chicken on the first side until golden brown, 6 to 7 minutes. Turn and continue to grill until the chicken is fully cooked, another 7 or 8 minutes. Serve with the eggplant stew.

INDIAN-STYLE EGGPLANT STEW

1 small Asian eggplant (about 6 oz)

1 tsp extra-virgin olive oil plus as need for brushing eggplant

Salt and freshly ground pepper as needed

SPICE BLEND

½ tsp garam masala

¼ tsp ground turmeric

¼ tsp ground cumin seeds

¼ tsp ground coriander

Pinch ground cayenne

Pinch ground clove

½ tsp finely chopped garlic

½ tsp grated ginger

½ serrano chile pepper, sliced thin

½ cup plain Greek yogurt

½ cup coarsely chopped tomatoes

2 tbsp chopped cilantro

1. Preheat broiler to high.

2. Cut the eggplant in half or quarters lengthwise, depending on its diameter, and then slice the eggplant crosswise ½-inch thick. Brush the eggplant with oil, and then season with salt and pepper. Broil until the eggplant has a rich brown color on both sides, turning once, about 8 minutes total. Set aside.

3. Combine all of the dry spices in a small bowl and set aside.

4. Heat 1 teaspoon of oil in a sauté pan over medium heat. Add the garlic and ginger. Cook, stirring constantly, until aromatic, about 15 seconds. Add the serrano chile and the dry spices, and stir until the spices are fragrant, about 30 seconds.

5. Add the eggplant and yogurt. Stir well to combine the ingredients, cover the pan, and reduce the heat to low. Simmer until the eggplant is tender, about 10 minutes. Add the tomatoes, and simmer 2 to 3 minutes. Remove the cover and simmer for a few minutes to cook away most of the liquid; the tomatoes should still retain their shape. Season with salt and pepper to taste. Sprinkle the eggplant with cilantro just before serving.

For contrast, add a refreshing salad made from thinly sliced cucumber and onion tossed with rice wine vinegar and seasoned with salt, pepper, and a pinch of sugar. Pita bread is a perfect accompaniment to mop up all of the juices.

brined pork chop with summer succotash

LISA: In the South, I can get fresh shell beans almost year-round. There are many different varieties, so I make this dish with whatever is available: butter beans, zipper peas, or black-eyed peas. Fortunately, succotash freezes well, so when fresh corn is in season, I make a large batch to freeze and have on hand as a quick dinner option.

MARK: Brining pork before cooking it produces a juicy, succulent chop. Ideally, you should start brining the night or morning before you'll be grilling. However, you can still make a great chop without this process by sprinkling both sides of the chop with ½ teaspoon salt an hour or two before cooking. Just before you put the chop on the grill, rinse the surface with cool water to remove the extra salt and blot the chop dry.

BRINED PORK CHOP

BRINE

1 tbsp salt

½ cup hot water

½ cup ice cubes, as needed

1 pork chop (about 6 oz)

1. To make the brine, combine the salt and hot water in a liquid measuring cup. Stir to dissolve the salt. Add enough ice to bring the total amount of brine to 1 cup. Pour the brine into a container, add the pork chop, cover, and marinate in the refrigerator at least 6 and up to 12 hours.

2. Preheat the grill to medium-high. Take the pork chop out of the brine and blot it dry with paper towels.

3. Grill the pork chop over direct heat turning once until browned on both sides, about 4 minutes total. Move the chop to indirect heat, and continue grilling until cooked through, turning once, another 4 minutes.

4. Spoon the succotash and its juices into a deep plate. Top the succotash with the pork chop and serve.

SUMMER SUCCOTASH

ADDING OVEN-DRIED TOMATOES to homey succotash gives this simple dish a modern twist and an unexpected burst of flavor.

1 cup Homemade Chicken Stock (page 134)

½ cup small lima beans, fresh or frozen

1 tsp extra-virgin olive oil

¼ cup finely chopped onion

1 ear corn, kernels cut from cob

8 pieces Oven-dried Tomatoes (page 141)

1 tbsp fresh chopped chives

Salt and freshly ground black pepper as needed

1. Bring the chicken stock to a boil in a saucepan over medium-high heat. Add the

lima beans and bring the stock back to a boil. Reduce the heat to low and simmer until the lima beans are tender to the bite, about 5 to 8 minutes. (The cooking time will vary depending on the size of beans and whether they are fresh or frozen.) Set the beans aside in their cooking liquid.

2. Heat the olive oil in a skillet over medium heat. Add the onions and sauté, stirring frequently, until they are tender and translucent, but not browned, about 3 minutes. Add the prepared lima beans with their cooking liquid and the corn kernels. Bring to simmer and cook over low heat until the corn is just tender, about 3 minutes.

3. Add the oven-dried tomatoes and cook until all of the ingredients are heated through. Add the chives, taste the succotash, and season with salt and pepper.

In defense of frozen lima beans, we think they are one of the few frozen vegetables that come close to fresh when cooked properly. Look for frozen baby limas if you can get them.

asian pork patties with lettuce wraps

THESE WRAPS WERE inspired by our trip to Vietnam with noted chef, Mai Pham, several years ago. We loved the "table salad" that accompanied many of the dishes we ate—essentially a platter of lettuce leaves, fresh herbs, and cucumbers. The salad ingredients are fresh and crunchy, while the meat and sauce contribute savory, salty, and sweet flavors for the perfect balance without any heaviness. Although we prefer the more traditional rice noodles, leftover rice from a previous night is an easy substitute.

The dipping sauce, *nuoc cham*, should be pungent with a pronounced flavor of salt, savory, and sweet. Good quality fish sauce (*nuoc nam*) is available at Asian markets and worth seeking out. You can find a variety of fresh Asian herbs at these markets, which are great to have if you cook a lot of Asian food. We grow our own Asian herbs, which is even more convenient and not at all difficult.

PORK PATTIES

¼ lb ground pork

3 tbsp finely chopped scallions

¾ tsp fish sauce (*nuoc nam*)

½ tsp finely grated fresh ginger

¼ tsp minced garlic

¼ tsp brown sugar

Salt and freshly ground pepper as needed

TABLE SALAD

5 large lettuce leaves (Boston, green leaf, or red leaf)

1 pickling cucumber, peeled, if desired, and sliced thin

Handful of fresh herbs: basil (preferably Asian variety),
    mint, cilantro

½ cup cooked rice stick noodles (rice vermicelli) or rice

Nuoc Cham (recipe follows)

1. Combine the pork, scallions, fish sauce, ginger, garlic, and brown sugar in a bowl. Add a pinch of salt and pepper and mix until the ingredients are evenly blended. Shape the mixture into 4 or 5 small oval patties and set aside in the refrigerator.

2. Put the ingredients for the table salad on a platter. Refrigerate until you are ready to eat.

3. Heat a grill to medium heat. Grill the patties over direct heat on the first side until lightly browned, about 3 minutes. Turn the patties once, and finish cooking on the second side, another 2 to 3 minutes. Remove to a platter and serve with the table salad and the *nuoc cham.*

4. This dish is assembled at the table. Place a lettuce leaf on your dinner plate and top with some rice noodles or rice, a generous spoonful of nuoc cham, a pork patty, some of the herbs, and sliced cucumber. Roll the lettuce leaf around the filling and eat. Repeat with the remaining patties.

NUOC CHAM

A LIGHT SPRINKLING of finely shredded carrots is a traditional garnish for *nuoc cham.*

1 Thai bird chile or ¼ serrano pepper, sliced thin

2 tsp sugar

½ tsp minced garlic

2 tbsp warm water

1 tbsp fish sauce (*nuoc nam*)

2 tsp fresh lime juice

1 tsp finely shredded carrots, optional

Reserve half of the sliced chile for garnish. Place the remaining chile into the bowl of a mortar and pestle. Add the sugar and garlic and pound to a paste. Stir in the water, fish sauce, and lime juice. Add the reserved chile slices. Garnish with the shredded carrots, if desired. The sauce is ready to serve now, or can be stored in the refrigerator up to 12 hours.

BAKED FRUIT GALETTES

LISA: To me, a galette is the perfect dessert and I never grow tired of it, whether I make it with plums, pluots, pears, or berries. During the winter, dried fruits make a nice filling when they are stewed in a little water or wine and sweetened with a touch of sugar.

I often use a coarse sugar, sometimes referred to as sanding sugar, to sprinkle on the galette before baking. The large granules add a nice crunch and a bit of sparkle. Sometimes I sprinkle a few nuts on top as well, before sprinkling on the sugar, to toast and caramelize while the galette bakes.

MARK: Our Quick Puff Pastry (page 143) is very easy to make and, in our opinion, far superior to anything you can buy. Once made, it can be cut into portion-size pieces, wrapped, and frozen so you can thaw out just what you need each time.

If you prefer, puff pastry can also be purchased, but be sure to look for one that is marked "Made with all butter." Pâte Brisée (page 143) is a suitable replacement, although it will not rise as high or be as flaky.

APPLE GALETTE

3 oz Quick Puff Pastry (page 143)

2 tsp Galette Base (page 61)

1 small apple, peeled, cored, sliced into ½-inch wedges (about ¾ cup)

2 tsp brown sugar

¼ tsp ground cinnamon

1 tsp Calvados, optional

1 tsp melted butter for brushing

1½ tsp granulated or coarse sugar for sprinkling

1. Preheat the oven to 400°F. Line a baking sheet with parchment paper.

2. Roll the puff pastry into a 6-inch circle, about ⅛ inch thick, and transfer it to the baking sheet. Sprinkle the galette base over the pastry, leaving a 1-inch border around the edge.

3. Toss the apples slices in a bowl with the brown sugar, cinnamon, and Calvados, if using, until evenly blended. Arrange the apple slices in a concentric circle over dough and base, leaving a ½-inch border of dough. Turn up the edge of dough, pinching it between your thumb and index finger to create small pleats that will hold the filling in place. Brush the dough and apples with the melted butter and sprinkle the galette with the sugar.

4. Bake the galette until browned, about 25 minutes. Serve warm.

PEACH AND RASPBERRY GALETTE

3 oz Quick Puff Pastry (page 143)

2 tsp Galette Base (recipe follows)

1 small peach, peeled, pitted, sliced into ½-inch wedges
     (about ½ cup)

10 raspberries

1 tsp melted butter for brushing

2½ tsp granulated or coarse sugar for sprinkling

1. Preheat the oven to 400°F. Line a baking sheet with parchment paper.

2. Roll the puff pastry into a 6-inch circle, about ⅛ inch thick, and transfer to the baking sheet. Sprinkle the base over the pastry, leaving a 1-inch border around the edge.

3. Pile the peaches over dough and base, leaving a ¾-inch border of dough. Top the peaches with raspberries. Turn up the edge of dough, pinching between your thumb and index finger to create small pleats that will hold the filling in place. Brush fruit and dough with butter and sprinkle with sugar.

4. Bake the galette until browned, about 25 minutes. Serve warm.

APRICOT GALETTE

3 oz Quick Puff Pastry (page 143)

2 tsp Galette Base (recipe follows)

2 apricots, peeled, pitted

1 tsp Amaretto, optional

1 tsp melted butter for brushing

2½ tsp granulated or coarse sugar for sprinkling

1. Preheat the oven to 400°F. Line a baking sheet with parchment paper.

2. Roll the puff pastry into a 6-inch circle, about ⅛ inch thick, and transfer to a baking sheet. Sprinkle the base over the pastry, leaving a 1-inch border around the edge.

3. Cut the apricots into halves or quarters, depending upon their size. Toss the apricots in a bowl with the amaretto until evenly coated. Place the apricots, cut side up, in a concentric circle over the dough and base, leaving a ½-inch border of dough. Turn up the edge of dough, pinching it between your thumb and index finger to create small pleats that will hold the filling in place. Brush the apricots and dough with the melted butter and sprinkle the galette with the sugar.

4. Bake the galette until browned, about 25 minutes. Serve warm.

GALETTE BASE

2 tbsp sugar

2 tbsp blanched slivered almonds, toasted

2 tbsp flour

Combine the sugar, almonds, and flour in a small food processor and process until nuts are finely ground. This base can be used for all baked fruit galettes, and this recipe makes enough for 8 or 9 galettes. Store any extra base in an airtight container in the freezer up to 4 weeks.

blackberry clafoutis

CLAFOUTIS IS TRADITIONALLY made with cherries, but it is every bit as good with a number of different fruits. This dessert is so versatile and easy to make that once you've tried it, you will probably find yourself making it regularly with whatever is in season. Try it with peaches and a hint of almond, pears with Sambuca or star anise, or raspberries and figs with framboise. A little whipped cream served on the side is a delicious accompaniment when you want to dress it up a bit.

⅔ cup large blackberries

1 tbsp framboise, or berry-flavored eau de vie

1 tbsp granulated sugar

CLAFOUTIS BATTER

1 piece vanilla bean (about 1½ inches)

⅓ cup milk or cream

1 egg

2 tbsp sugar

1 tbsp all-purpose flour

1½ tsp melted butter plus as needed for brushing the
   baking dish

Confectioner's sugar for dusting

1. Preheat the oven to 350°F. Butter a 1-cup gratin or shallow baking dish.

2. Dip the blackberries quickly and gently in bowl of cold water. Lift them from the water and let them drain on a few layers of paper towels. Transfer the berries to a bowl, add the framboise and sugar, and toss gently to coat the berries. Set them aside to macerate for 10 to 15 minutes.

3. To make the batter, split the vanilla bean lengthwise and scrape the seeds into a small bowl. Add the milk or cream, egg, sugar, flour, and butter. Whisk until you have a smooth batter.

4. Spoon the berries out of the sugary syrup and into the bottom of the prepared dish. Pour the batter over the berries, and then bake in the oven for about 30 minutes until browned and puffed. Serve warm or at room temperature with a light sifting of confectioner's sugar over the top.

PEACHES IN LEMON VERBENA SYRUP

MARK: This is a nice way to serve dessert without adding a lot of calories or heaviness to a meal. The sugar and flavoring in the syrup help to bring out the essence of a perfect piece of fruit. The syrup can be made several days in advance and rewarmed in the microwave before you add the fruit.

LISA: You can flavor your poaching syrup with different herbs, liquors, or spices depending upon the fruit you want to poach, the season, and your preference. We have several fruit trees in our garden in Atlanta, so I've developed a number of adaptations to enjoy poached fruits in every season. I tend to make extra and eat it with yogurt for breakfast the next day. Here are a few of my favorites:

- Plums make a good substitute for the peaches.

- Try an apple or pear with cinnamon or vanilla bean in the fall. You will need to cook these fruits in the syrup for a minute to soften them slightly.

- Orange slices are delicious in the winter added to a warm star anise or lime syrup.

- Mix fresh berries and a touch of cassis into the syrup after it has cooled slightly.

POACHING SYRUP

½ cup water

2 tbsp white wine

1½ tbsp sugar

1 tsp fresh lemon juice

One 6-inch sprig lemon verbena

1 fresh peach, peeled, pitted, and sliced into ¾-inch wedges

1. In a 1-quart glass measuring cup, combine the water, wine, sugar, and lemon juice. Microwave on high until the mixture comes to a boil, stopping and stirring a few times to dissolve the sugar. Once the boil is reached, continue to microwave for 2½ more minutes. Add the lemon verbena sprig and microwave for 30 seconds. The mixture should have a syrupy consistency.

2. Add the peach wedges to the syrup, cover with plastic wrap, and let them steep at room temperature for 20 to 30 minutes. Remove lemon verbena sprig and serve the peaches with the syrup.

CHAPTER THREE

Fall

the fall pantry

FALL IS ONE of the best times of the year to cook. Sturdy cooking greens, lettuce, and spinach are back in season, potatoes are starting to mature, and raspberries produce a second harvest.

VEGETABLES	Kale	Turnips
Avocado	Kohlrabi	Yams
Beets	Mustard greens	Winter squash
Bok choy	Mushrooms	Zucchini
Broccoli	Okra	
Brussels sprouts	Onions	FRUITS
Cabbage	Peppers	Apples
Carrots	Potatoes	Cranberry
Cauliflower	Pumpkins	Dates
Celeriac	Purslane	Grapes
Chard	Radicchio	Pears
Chiles	Rutabaga	Persimmons
Collard greens	Scallions	Pomegranate
Daikon	Shallots	Plums
Fennel	Sweet potatoes	Raspberries
Garlic	Tomatoes	
Horseradish	Tomatillos	

spinach salad with chèvre, raspberry vinaigrette, and candied pecans

MARK: Chèvre is a fresh, tangy goat cheese, the perfect creamy companion to tart berries and savory nuts. Try fresh peaches or apricots instead of the raspberries for a different, but equally good, combination. Serve this as an entrée or as the first course for a fall dinner followed by something from the grill.

LISA: Most of this recipe can be prepped ahead of time, making for a quick dinner after a busy day. The spinach can be washed and spun dry several days ahead. You can make the salad dressing and candied pecans in advance as well (this recipe makes more than you'll need for one serving).

SPINACH SALAD WITH CHÈVRE

4 cups spinach leaves, lightly packed

2 or 3 tbsp Raspberry Vinaigrette, as needed (recipe follows)

½ cup raspberries

1½ oz crumbled chèvre

2 or 3 tbsp Candied Pecans (recipe follows) or other
    toasted nuts

Toss the spinach together with the raspberry vinaigrette in a salad bowl. Add the raspberries, half of the chèvre, and half of the pecans. Toss the salad gently once or twice to coat all of the ingredients and serve the salad at once topped with the remaining chèvre and pecans.

RASPBERRY VINAIGRETTE

THE QUANTITY OF honey used in the dressing will depend on the acidity of the raspberry vinegar used. Some fruit vinegars tend to be a bit sweet and others have no perceptible sweetness whatsoever.

1 tbsp minced shallot

2 tbsp raspberry vinegar

Salt and freshly ground pepper as needed

½ tsp Dijon-style mustard

½ tsp honey (or as needed)

2 tbsp walnut oil

1 tbsp canola oil

In a small bowl, combine the shallot, vinegar, and a pinch of salt and pepper. Let rest for 15 minutes. Whisk in the mustard, honey, and oils. Taste the vinaigrette and season with more honey as desired, but resist making the dressing too syrupy sweet.

CANDIED PECANS

¼ cup pecan pieces

2 tsp honey

1 tsp canola oil

Pinch salt

Pinch cayenne pepper

1. Preheat the oven to 350°F.

2. Combine the pecans with the honey, oil, salt, and cayenne in a small bowl. Spread the nuts out in an even layer on a nonstick pan sprayed with cooking spray or lined with Silpat or parchment. Bake, turning once, until toasted, about 20 minutes. Remove from the oven and let cool on the pan.

3. Break the pecans into smaller pieces, if desired, once they are cool enough to handle. Store the pecans at room temperature in an airtight container until needed.

steak salad with potatoes, mushrooms, and blue cheese

LISA: We love steak, particularly New York Strip. There are many other cuts you might try: shell steak, rib eye, porterhouse, or sirloin all work in this dish. For the best flavor and texture, buy a 1-inch-thick steak and cut it to size—you can freeze the unused portion.

This salad combines a traditional steak dinner all in one bowl with delicious results. Add a glass of red wine, and dinner is complete.

MARK: The lettuces listed in the recipe have a firm texture to hold up to the slightly warm vegetables and steak. They are a fall/winter seasonal mix, which goes well with the mushrooms, fennel, and blue cheese. There are many varieties of mushrooms; any will work with this dish from standard white mushrooms to cremini or chanterelles, depending upon both the season and your budget.

3 oz fingerling or small new potatoes, scrubbed

Salt and freshly ground pepper as needed

1½ tsp finely chopped shallots

½ tsp balsamic vinegar

4 oz New York strip steak, cut 1 inch thick

½ tsp olive oil

½ cup sliced cremini mushrooms

SALAD

4 cups mixed salad greens (frisée, arugula, radicchio, spinach, and Belgian endive)

¼ cup diced fresh fennel or celery

¼ cup thinly sliced red pepper

½ oz blue cheese

1 tbsp chopped chives

2 or 3 tbsp Balsamic Vinaigrette to taste (page 138)

1. Put the potatoes in a small pot and add enough cold water to cover. Season the water with salt and bring to boil over high heat. Reduce the heat to low and simmer, partially covered, until the potatoes are just tender when pierced with the tip of a

paring knife, about 12 minutes. Drain the potatoes and cut them into halves or quarters, depending on their size. Toss them together with the shallots and vinegar in a salad bowl and set aside.

2. Preheat the oven to 400°F.

3. Season the steak with salt and pepper. Heat the olive oil in a small sauté pan over medium-high heat. Add the steak and cook, undisturbed, on the first side until well-browned, about 3 minutes.

4. Turn the steak and add the mushrooms, scattering them around the sides of the steak. Season the mushrooms with salt and pepper. Cook the steak on the second side until browned, about 2 more minutes.

Turn the mushrooms, then transfer the pan to the oven to finish cooking the steak to your preferred doneness, about 3 minutes for medium-rare.

5. Remove the meat to a plate and let it rest for 5 minutes. Add the reserved potato and shallot mixture to the mushrooms in the pan and stir to release any drippings from the pan. Season with salt and pepper.

6. Combine the salad greens, fennel or celery, red pepper, blue cheese, and chives in a salad bowl. Add the potato-mushroom mixture and the balsamic vinaigrette. Toss to coat the greens evenly and place on a dinner plate. Slice the steak and fan over the salad.

SWISS CHARD AND WHITE BEAN SOUP

LISA: This is a hearty, cold weather soup, both rich and satisfying. Best of all, it's loaded with dark greens and legumes that are on the "A list" of healthy eating choices. The finishing touch of olive oil and Parmesan cheese is a delicious addition to round out the flavors. Because this soup is even better the next day and also freezes well, we wrote the recipe to serve two. It's a satisfying lunch on a cool day.

MARK: Swiss chard cooks quickly and has a mild flavor. If you purchase more Swiss chard than you need, you can use it in our recipe for Sausage and Fig Skewers (page 89) or as a substitute for the greens called for in the Mediterranean Rice Salad (page 33) or Penne with Broccoli Rabe and Garlic (page 113).

MAKES 2 SERVINGS

1 tbsp olive oil

⅔ cup diced onion

1 small carrot, diced small

1 garlic clove, chopped

3½ oz cleaned and chopped Swiss chard (about 3 cups)

1½ cups cooked white beans (page 136)

3 cups Homemade Chicken Stock (page 134)

3 tbsp slivered sun-dried or Oven-dried Tomatoes (page 141)

Salt and freshly ground pepper as needed

GARNISH

1 tsp extra-virgin olive oil

1 tbsp freshly grated Parmesan

1. Heat the oil in a medium saucepot over low heat. Add the onion and carrot and sauté until the onion is translucent and the vegetables soften, about 4 minutes. Add the garlic and cook for 1 minute.

2. Add the chard and white beans. Stir to coat the chard with the oil. Continue to cook, stirring occasionally, until the chard has wilted, about 2 minutes. Add the stock and bring the soup to a boil over high heat. Reduce the heat to low and simmer until the soup is flavorful and all of the ingredients are fully cooked, about 20 minutes.

3. Add the sun-dried or oven-dried tomatoes to the soup. Taste and season the soup with salt and pepper. Serve at once in a heated bowl drizzled with a little extra-virgin olive oil and a spoonful of grated Parmesan, if desired.

black bean falafel with tahini sauce

OUR VERSION OF the traditional Middle Eastern sandwich is made from cooked black beans rather than the traditional uncooked garbanzo beans, which can take up to 24 hours of soaking time. This recipe is yet another way we have found to take advantage of a batch of home-cooked beans (although, you can use canned black beans if necessary).

BLACK BEAN FALAFEL

½ cup cooked black beans (page 136)

1 tbsp dried bread crumbs

1 tbsp chopped parsley

1½ tsp chopped cilantro

1½ tsp lemon juice

¾ tsp minced garlic

⅛ tsp ground cumin

⅛ tsp ground coriander

Pinch cayenne

Salt and freshly ground pepper as needed

2 tbsp finely chopped onion

⅓ cup canola oil, or as needed for frying

GARNISHES:

Whole wheat pita bread, warmed and halved

Shredded lettuce (romaine or green leaf)

Tomato and cucumber slices

Tahini Sauce (recipe follows)

1. Combine the black beans, bread crumbs, parsley, cilantro, lemon juice, garlic, cumin, coriander, cayenne, salt, and pepper in a food processor. Process until the ingredients are finely chopped, but not a paste. Add the onion and pulse the food processor on and off once or twice, just until the onion is blended. Form the mixture into 2 or 3 patties.

2. Heat a small sauté pan over medium heat with enough oil to come to a depth of ¼ inch. When the oil is hot, add the bean patties and cook until browned on both sides, turning once, 4 to 5 minutes total. Blot the patties briefly on paper towels. Serve the falafels very hot in the warmed pita bread with the garnishes and tahini sauce.

TAHINI SAUCE

IF YOU DO not want to buy an entire can of tahini for the sauce, you can substitute peanut butter instead.

2 tbsp tahini paste (sesame seed paste)

1 tbsp water or yogurt

1½ tsp lemon juice

⅛ tsp chopped garlic, mashed with salt

Salt and freshly ground pepper as needed

Make tahini sauce by whisking all ingredients together in a small bowl. Set aside or store in a covered container in the refrigerator for up to 2 days.

salad sandwich wraps

WRAP SANDWICHES HAVE never lost their appeal. Using a freshly baked flatbread changes this deli and lunch counter favorite into a satisfying lunch or dinner for one. We've offered some suggestions here to vary the filling as well as to streamline the preparation of the flatbread.

LISA: This is our version of the popular flatbread sandwich wrap. It is as satisfying as pizza, but much lighter because the fillings are salads made with lots of vegetables and just a bit of protein or cheese. You can substitute warmed pita bread, lavash or naan for the flatbread.

MARK: If your dough is already made and in the freezer, remember to take it out of the freezer in the morning and let it thaw in the refrigerator during the day. About an hour before you plan to bake it, remove it from the refrigerator to warm to room temperature while your oven preheats. (Your pizza stone will take about that long to heat properly.) The dough can also be cooked on a charcoal grill over medium direct heat until blistered and browned on both sides; it takes about 2 minutes per side.

One 6-oz ball Pizza Dough (page 142), room temperature

1 tbsp olive oil, as needed for brushing

Kosher or sea salt as needed

Salad Filling (recipes follow)

1. Place a pizza stone on the bottom rack of the oven. Preheat the oven to 450°F. Preheat a baking sheet pan in the oven while you prepare the dough.

2. Roll or stretch the dough into a 9-inch circle. Remove the baking sheet from the oven and quickly brush it with oil. Transfer the dough to the baking sheet. Brush the top of dough with a little oil and season it with salt. Set the pan on the pizza stone and bake until golden brown, 6 to 7 minutes. Immediately remove the flatbread from the pan and wrap it in a clean cloth towel for 2 minutes. (This keeps the flatbread pliable enough to roll up.)

3. Place the flatbread on a large square of parchment paper (about 16 inches square). Spoon the salad filling onto the flatbread. Roll the filling up inside the flatbread, wrapping the entire sandwich with the parchment to hold it together. Serve at once.

GREEK SALAD FILLING

Combine 1½ cups chopped romaine, 2 oz feta cheese, and 3 or 4 pitted kalamata olives with as many of the following as you like: diced tomato, fresh or roasted pepper strips, sliced or diced cucumbers, red onion, grated carrots. Finish the salad with shredded mint and parsley. Toss with Greek Salad Dressing (page 139).

CHICKEN CAESAR FILLING

Combine 1½ cups chopped romaine with 1 or 2 mashed anchovy fillets, 1 or 2 tablespoons shaved or grated Parmesan, and 3 ounces of diced cooked chicken. Toss with Lemon-Garlic Salad Dressing (page 139).

NIÇOISE FILLING

Combine 1½ cups chopped romaine with 2 or 3 ounces of oil-packed tuna, a chopped hard boiled egg, diced tomatoes, 4 or 5 pitted Niçoise olives, and ⅓ cup steamed green beans. Toss the salad with Balsamic or Classic Vinaigrette (page 138).

asian chicken and cabbage salad

THIS FLAVORFUL SALAD is a meal on its own. The chicken breast can be poached a day ahead or cooked pork or shrimp can be used, alone or in combination. The shallots can be made a few days ahead.

1 piece boneless chicken breast (about 4 oz)

DRESSING

½ tsp finely minced garlic

½ tsp finely chopped Serrano chile

1 tsp fish sauce

1½ tbsp lime juice

2 tsp sugar

1 tbsp water

Salt as needed

CABBAGE SALAD

1 cup very thinly sliced cabbage, preferably sliced on
    a mandoline

1 carrot, peeled and cut into very thin 3-inch-long julienne,
    preferably cut on a mandoline

1 scallion, very thinly sliced into 3-inch-long julienne

⅛ red pepper, cut into 3-inch-long thin julienne

¼ cup thinly sliced seeded cucumber

¼ cup cilantro leaves

1 tbsp fried shallot (purchased or see note at right)

1 tbsp chopped roasted peanuts

1. Place the chicken in small pot, cover with cold water, and add a little salt for seasoning. Cover the pot and set over low heat. As soon as water starts to boil, turn the heat off and let the chicken sit, covered, in the hot water until cooked through, about 6 minutes. Remove the chicken from the water and set it aside to cool. When cool, slice the chicken into thin, bite-size strips.

2. Make the dressing by mixing together the garlic, chile, fish sauce, lime juice, sugar, water, and a pinch of salt. Set aside.

3. Combine the cabbage, carrot, scallion, and pepper in a large bowl and cover with ice water. Let sit for 30 minutes, and then drain well and pat dry with paper towels.

4. Return the cabbage mixture to the bowl and add the chicken, cucumber, and cilantro. Toss with the dressing. Serve in a shallow bowl or plate, sprinkled with fried shallot and peanuts.

FRIED SHALLOT

Slice 1 large shallot crosswise into thin slices, place them on a paper towel, and blot to remove the excess moisture. Let the slices air-dry for 30 minutes. Heat oil to a depth of ¼ inch in a small pan over low heat. When hot, add the shallot slices and cook very slowly, stirring and watching carefully, until just golden, about 6 minutes. Remove them with a slotted spoon to paper towels to drain briefly. Season with salt.

chèvre soufflé with broccoli salad

MARK: A supper that features eggs can be a mainstay of the single cook, but instead of a plain fried egg on toast or scrambled egg with cheese, we turn to a savory soufflé. Because the recipe for the base makes enough for two soufflés, you can enjoy it now and again in a few weeks. The second soufflé is a snap to put together, since the base is already done.

LISA: The broccoli salad is a nice pairing with the chèvre soufflé. The brightly colored lettuces and crisp textures complement the creamy soufflé. However, a plain green salad would be a quick and suitable substitute

MAKES 2 SOUFFLÉS

1½ tbsp butter

1½ tbsp all purpose flour

½ cup milk, heated

Salt as needed

Small pinch of cayenne pepper, to taste

A few grains of freshly grated nutmeg, to taste

2 egg yolks

2 oz crumbled chèvre, divided

¾ tsp fresh chopped thyme

Butter, as needed for coating

Finely grated Parmesan, as needed for coating

3 egg whites, lightly beaten

Pinch cream of tartar

Dried thyme

1. To make the soufflé base, prepare a roux with the flour and butter as follows: melt the butter in a medium saucepot over medium heat until the butter foams. Reduce the heat to low, add the flour, and continue to cook, stirring constantly for 1 minute. Do not let the flour brown.

2. Add the milk and whisk until there are no lumps. Season with a pinch of salt, cayenne, and nutmeg. Increase the heat to medium and bring the mixture to a full boil. Continue to cook, whisking constantly, until the mixture is very thick and smooth, about 1 minute. Remove the mixture from the heat.

3. Place the egg yolks in a bowl, and gradually whisk the hot mixture into the yolks. (Add the hot milk mixture just a spoonful or two at a time at first to temper the yolks.) Once you've added about one-third of the hot mixture to the yolks, you can add the remainder all at once.

4. Divide the soufflé base between two containers and add half of the the chèvre and fresh thyme to each portion of the base. At this point the soufflé base is ready to finish (step 6) or it can be wrapped and stored in the refrigerator for up to 3 days or the freezer for 4 weeks.

5. Divide the egg whites between two containers. If you are not making the soufflés now, wrap the egg whites well and store in the refrigerator for up to 3 days or the freezer for up to 4 weeks.

6. To finish the soufflé, bring one container of soufflé base and one container of egg whites to room temperature.

7. Preheat the oven to 400°F and set the rack in the middle third. Butter the inside of a 12-ounce soufflé dish. Sprinkle the bottom and sides of the dish with Parmesan, coating the inside completely. Set aside.

8. Whip the egg whites with a pinch of cream of tartar and salt until stiff peaks form. Gently fold the egg whites into the soufflé base with a rubber spatula until evenly blended, and then spoon into the prepared soufflé cup. (Work carefully so you don't get drips on the rim and sides. If you do have drips, take the time to wipe them away or your soufflé will not rise as much as it could.) Top the soufflé with a light sprinkling of dried thyme.

9. Put the soufflé in the oven and immediately turn the heat down to 375°F. Bake until the soufflé is puffed, browned, and just set, about 15 minutes. Serve immediately with the broccoli salad.

SOUFFLÉ VARIATIONS

One soufflé can usually take on about ¼ cup of added ingredients. Here are some suggested soufflé variations instead of the chèvre and thyme called for in this version. A sauté of onions, peppers, and prosciutto paired with Fontina; chopped spinach sautéed with shallots and dill paired with feta cheese; or aged cheddar with smothered green onions.

BROCCOLI SALAD

2 oz broccoli, washed, peeled, sliced on a diagonal into
   1-inch pieces

2 mushrooms, wiped clean and sliced thin

1 tbsp slivered fennel

1 tbsp toasted chopped walnuts

1 cup bite-size mixture of radicchio, Belgian endive,
   and watercress

Walnut Oil Vinaigrette, as needed (page 139)

1. Blanch the broccoli in boiling salted water for 1 minute. Drain in a colander and rinse under cold water. Drain and pat dry with a paper towel.

2. Place remaining salad ingredients and broccoli in salad bowl. Just before the soufflé comes out of the oven, toss the salad with the dressing, and serve immediately alongside the soufflé.

leek and blue cheese tart

MARK: With a little advance prep, this meal can be put together very quickly. The pâte brisée can be made and frozen well in advance, and the leek and mushroom mixture can be made a day or two ahead. Then all you need to do is roll out the dough, add the filling, and bake. Serve it with a salad of mixed winter greens such as frisée, radicchio, arugula, and butter lettuces for a satisfying fall brunch or dinner.

LISA: This recipe is a great vehicle to enjoy the last bit of cheese; try chèvre, Gruyère, Edam, Monterey Jack, Brie, or whatever you have on hand. Thinly sliced onions can stand in for the leeks.

1 tsp unsalted butter

1 large leek, quartered lengthwise and sliced into ribbons

2 cremini mushrooms, quartered and sliced thin

½ tsp chopped thyme

Salt and freshly ground pepper as needed

2 tsp white wine

3 Niçoise olives, pitted and chopped

One portion (2½ oz) Pâte Brisée (page 143)

¾ oz crumbled blue cheese (about 2 tbsp)

1½ tsp chopped walnuts

1. Melt the butter in a small sauté pan over medium-low heat. Add the leek, reduce the heat to low, cover the pan, and stew the leek slowly, stirring from time to time, until tender, about 4 minutes. Add the mushrooms and thyme, season with salt and pepper, and continue to cook, covered, until the mushrooms release their juices.

2. Uncover the pan, add the wine, and continue to cook until the wine cooks away and the mushrooms start to brown, about 4 minutes. Transfer to a bowl and cool to room temperature. Stir in the olives, taste, and then season with salt and pepper.

3. Preheat the oven to 400°F.

4. On a floured surface roll the pâte brisée to an 8-inch circle. Transfer the dough to a parchment-lined baking sheet. Spoon the leek filling over the pastry, leaving a 1-inch border. Sprinkle the blue cheese over the filling. Fold the pastry up over the outer edge of the leek filling, pinching it at 1-inch intervals to form a rustic circle. Sprinkle the walnuts over the filling.

5. Bake the tart for about 20 minutes, until the pastry is golden brown. Serve warm or room temperature.

butternut squash risotto

LISA: When the cool weather arrives, I think of this risotto as the perfect comfort food to enjoy as an entrée or an accompaniment to braised or roasted meats and poultry dishes. As a main course, serve it with a leafy green vegetable, like kale or broccoli rabe, blanched for one minute in salted water and drained, and then sautéed with olive oil, garlic, a few flakes of crushed red pepper flakes, and a touch of anchovy paste.

MARK: The two key ingredients for a good risotto are the right rice and a high-quality stock. Risotto deserves your own homemade stock. Choose a medium-grain, round rice like Arborio, or Carnaroli for a creamy risotto. The shape of this rice, as well as the type of starch it contains, means that the grains will absorb large amounts of liquid as well as release enough of their own starch to produce a flowing consistency (*all'onde* or wavelike).

SERVES 1 AS MAIN COURSE OR 2 AS A SIDE DISH

1½ cups Homemade Chicken Stock (page 134)

1 tsp unsalted butter

1 tsp olive oil

9 fresh sage leaves or a 2-inch sprig of rosemary

¼ cup diced onion

⅓ cup Arborio or Carnaroli rice

½ cup grated butternut squash (medium grate)

1 tbsp white wine

¼ cup grated Parmesan cheese

Salt and freshly ground pepper as needed

1 or 2 slices (¾ oz) Prosciutto ham, cut into ribbons

1. Place the chicken stock in a small saucepan and bring it to a simmer over medium heat. Keep the stock warm.

2. In a second saucepan, heat the butter and olive oil over medium heat. Add the sage leaves to the pan and sauté until the foam subsides and the leaves are light brown and crisp, about 2 minutes. Lift the leaves from the oil with a fork or slotted spoon; set them aside on a paper towel to drain and cool.

3. Add the onion to the oil remaining in the pan and sauté, stirring frequently, until translucent but not brown, 2 to 3 minutes.

4. Add the rice and stir with a wooden spoon over low heat until the rice is well coated and lightly fried but not browned, about 2 minutes. Add the grated butternut squash, increase the heat to medium, and stir to combine the squash and the rice, about 1 minute.

5. Add the wine and stir it into the rice, and then add ⅓ cup of the heated chicken stock. Cook over medium-low heat, stirring constantly, until the rice completely absorbs the stock, about 5 minutes. Add ⅓ cup of the heated stock, and cook, stirring constantly, until absorbed, about 5 minutes. Add ⅓ cup of stock and cook, still stirring, until the stock is absorbed and the rice tender but still has a bit of bite at the center, another 5 minutes.

6. Add enough of the remaining stock for a porridge-like consistency. Remove the pan from the heat and stir in the Parmesan cheese. Taste and season with salt and pepper, if needed.

7. Serve the risotto immediately topped with the ribbons of prosciutto ham. Crumble the fried sage leaves over the top, and top with additional Parmesan if desired.

Leftover butternut squash can be cut into chunks, tossed with olive oil and seasonings such as garlic, salt, pepper, and thyme sprigs, and then roasted on a baking sheet in a 375°F oven until tender and edges are browned, about 30 minutes. Serve the roasted squash as a vegetable side dish or purée it with chicken stock to make a simple and flavorful soup.

CURRIED CHICKPEAS

LISA: One taste of this Thai-inspired curry will convince you that it is well worth the time and effort involved in making your own green curry paste. The fresh, light flavor is far superior to any of the prepared curry pastes you might find at the grocery store. In addition to using it for this recipe, try it as a rub for meat skewers (satays) or added to dressings for salads that include ingredients like mango or Asian noodles.

MARK: This recipe is a basic blueprint from which you can create many different dishes, such as using shrimp or chicken instead of chickpeas or serving the curry over noodles rather than steamed rice. If the chickpeas are soaked and cooked ahead, this is quick to put together. In a pinch, feel free to use canned chickpeas that have been rinsed and drained.

CURRIED CHICKPEAS

3 green onions

1 tsp canola oil

1½ tsp Thai Green Curry Paste (recipe follows)

¾ cup cooked chickpeas (page 136)

½ cup lite coconut milk (or ¼ cup regular coconut milk and ¼ cup water)

2 tsp peanut butter

1½ tsp fish sauce (*nam pla* or *nuoc nam*)

½ small tomato, cut into 6 wedges

½ tsp lime juice

Cilantro leaves for garnish

Steamed Jasmine Rice (page 136)

1. Trim the green onions. Cut away the green tops, slice thinly, and reserve separately

to garnish the curry. Slice the white portion of the green onions thinly.

2. Heat the canola oil in a medium sauté pan or saucepan over medium-low heat. Add the sliced white portions of the green onions and sauté, stirring constantly, until tender but not browned, about 1 minute.

3. Add the curry paste and cook, stirring constantly, until it is lightly fried and fragrant but not browned, about 1 minute. Add the chickpeas, lite coconut milk (or coconut milk and water), peanut butter, and fish sauce. Simmer over low heat until slightly reduced and thickened, 4 or 5 minutes.

4. Add the tomato wedges to the curry and continue to simmer until the tomatoes are heated through, about 3 minutes. Taste and season with lime juice.

5. Serve the curry over the steamed jasmine rice topped with the sliced green onion tops and cilantro leaves.

THAI GREEN CURRY PASTE

MAKES ½ CUP

1½ tsp coriander seeds

¼ tsp cumin seeds

12 black peppercorns

4 green Thai bird chiles, minced (or 8 jalapeño peppers)

¼ cup packed whole fresh cilantro leaves and stems

¼ cup packed fresh whole basil leaves

1 tbsp minced fresh ginger

1½ tsp minced garlic

One 2-inch piece lemongrass, white parts only, minced finely

Grated zest of ½ lime

2 tbsp canola oil

1. In a small, heavy skillet combine the coriander seeds, cumin seeds, and peppercorns. Heat over medium-low heat, stirring occasionally to lightly toast the spices. Let cool, and then using a spice grinder, or mortar and pestle, grind the spices fine and set aside.

2. In a small food processor, combine the chiles, cilantro, basil, ginger, garlic, lemongrass, and lime zest and process to a paste.

3. Add the ground toasted spices and, with the machine running, drizzle in the oil to make a paste. Add a little more oil, if necessary, to process. Use immediately or store in a small container covered with a plastic wrap to seal the surface. The paste will keep for up to 1 month in the refrigerator.

oven-roasted snapper with potatoes, tomatoes, and olives

THIS IS A good recipe for the fall, when you tire of summer's fish steaks from the grill, and want a meal with lots of flavor and little preparation. Serve this dish with spinach and chickpeas quickly sautéed in olive oil with a bit of garlic and crushed red pepper flakes. Different fish would be suitable with this dish—sea bass, grouper, and swordfish to name a few.

5 oz russet or Yukon gold potatoes, peeled and cut into ¼-inch-thick slices

2½ tsp extra-virgin olive oil, divided use

½ garlic clove, sliced

¼ tsp finely chopped rosemary

Salt and freshly ground pepper as needed

4 cherry tomatoes, halved

3 kalamata olives, pitted and halved

3 thin lemon slices, preferably Meyer lemon

1 piece red snapper fillet (about 5 oz)

1 tbsp white wine

1 tbsp water

1 tsp lemon juice

1. Preheat the oven to 425°F.

2. Toss the potatoes together with 1½ teaspoons of olive oil, garlic, rosemary, salt, and pepper in a small roasting pan. Roast until the potatoes are nearly tender, about 10 minutes. Add the tomatoes and olives, mix to combine them with the potatoes, and spread in an even layer.

3. Arrange the lemon slices in the center of the potato mixture, overlapping them. Place the fish fillet on top of lemon slices, skin side up. Add the wine, water, and lemon juice. Drizzle the remaining 1 teaspoon of olive oil over the fish and season with salt and pepper.

4. Bake the fish until is just cooked through and opaque, about 15 minutes, depending on how thick your fish fillet is.

5. Serve the fish on a warm plate with the vegetables and spoon the pan juices over everything.

spiced halibut with chickpea salad

FLAVORS FROM ALL over the Mediterranean combine to make this a fresh and healthy meal. For variation, try this recipe using lamb chops or a chicken breast in place of the halibut.

LISA: Preparing chickpeas from the dried form produces a superior product. Although it does require some advance planning, they are easy to prepare and, once cooked, can be refrigerated for several days or frozen for a few weeks. In addition to the recipes in this book that call for them, you can toss them into a salad, make a quick hummus for a dip, or follow my lead and double the recipe for this salad to have for lunch the next day with a piece of warmed pita bread.

SPICED HALIBUT

1 piece halibut filet (about 5 oz)

½ tsp ground coriander

½ tsp ground cumin

¼ tsp sweet paprika

Salt and freshly ground pepper as needed

½ tsp olive oil

1. Wash the halibut and pat dry. Combine the spices in a shallow bowl. Dredge the fish on both sides in the spice mix.

2. Heat the olive oil in a small nonstick sauté pan over medium heat. When the oil is hot, add the halibut and sauté on the first side until lightly golden, about 4 minutes. Turn the halibut and cook on the second side until the fish is just opaque in the center, another 3 to 4 minutes.

3. Serve the halibut accompanied by the chickpea salad.

CHICKPEA SALAD

⅔ cup cooked and drained chickpeas (page 136)

6 quartered cherry tomatoes or 1 small tomato, cut into thin wedges

2 tbsp thin slivers sweet onion, such as Vidalia

2 tbsp roughly torn mint leaves

2 tbsp roughly torn Italian parsley leaves

¼ tsp minced garlic

1 tbsp extra-virgin olive oil

Juice and zest of ¼ lemon, or to taste

Salt and freshly ground pepper as needed

Combine the salad ingredients in a small bowl. Let the salad rest at room temperature while you prepare the fish. The salad will keep for up to 24 hours in the refrigerator.

roasted duck with orange sauce and multigrain pilaf with dried cranberries and walnuts

LISA: Boneless duck breast makes a quick, elegant meal. It can usually be found in the meat case at specialty markets. I've used the breast from a Long Island ducking in this recipe; it is perfectly sized to make one portion. Serve the duck with the pilaf recipe below and sautéed spinach or steamed French green beans for added color.

MARK: If I've made a braised dish like the Braised Short Ribs on page 92 , I always freeze the leftover sauce and use it instead of chicken stock when finishing a pan sauce. It adds a rich dimension to this dish. Of course, the flavors in the braising sauce should always be compatible with the dish being made, never overwhelming it with added spices or different flavors.

ROASTED DUCK WITH ORANGE SAUCE

1 portion boneless duck breast, trimmed, approximately 6 oz

1½ tsp julienned orange zest (page 29)

1 tsp red wine vinegar

1 tsp red wine

1 tsp honey

¼ cup Homemade Chicken Stock (page 134)

½ tsp Grand Marnier

1. Score the skin of the duck with a sharp knife at ¾ inch intervals being careful not to cut into the meat. You can also discard the skin completely, if desired. Season with salt and pepper.

2. Blanch the zest in a small pot of boiling water for 1 minute and drain. Rinse under cold water to stop cooking process, Drain, pat dry with a paper towel, and set aside. Heat a small sauté pan over medium heat. Add the duck breast and cook on the skin side first for 5 minutes. Turn and cook for another 4 minutes for medium-rare. (A skinless breast cooks more quickly.) Remove to a plate and set aside while making the sauce.

3. Pour the excess fat from pan. Deglaze the pan with vinegar, red wine, and honey, stirring until reduced by two-thirds, about 2 minutes. Add the stock, bring to a boil, and simmer until reduced by about half, 2 minutes. Add the Grand Marnier, remove from the heat, and adjust the seasoning with salt and pepper.

4. Slice duck on slight angle into 3 or 4 slices and fan on to plate. Sprinkle some of the orange zest over the duck and add the rest to the sauce. Spoon the sauce around the duck (not over the crispy skin if you have chosen to keep it). Serve immediately with multigrain pilaf.

MULTIGRAIN PILAF

THIS HEALTHY WHOLE grain pilaf goes well with many foods, and different garnishes can be added for variety. It can be cooked and chilled a few days in advance. Reheat and add the garnishes just before serving.

½ tsp butter

1 scallion or ½ shallot, chopped

½ cup cooked multigrain pilaf or whole grain rice mix, unseasoned and cooked according to package directions

1 tbsp chopped toasted walnuts

1 tbsp dried cranberries

Salt and freshly ground pepper as needed

Heat a small nonstick pan over medium-low heat with the butter. When melted, add the scallion and cook about 1 minute, until just tender. Add the rice and warm through. Add the walnuts and cranberries. Season with salt and pepper.

grilled quail with pancetta and mushrooms, polenta, and sautéed spinach

LISA: This beautiful dinner features all of the foods we start to yearn for in the fall—game birds like quail, cool weather spinach, and hearty, comforting polenta.

MARK: Quail can be purchased in small quantities, so it is ideal for a "one-person" meal. We cook with it often as it is available fresh year-round in Georgia. It is typically sold frozen in other parts of the country, although specialty butchers may have fresh quail for short periods of time in the fall. A frozen quail will thaw safely overnight in the refrigerator. Before you leave for work, marinate the quail so it's ready for the grill when you get home. If you have any leftover brown sauce or juices from a stew in your freezer, use that instead of the chicken stock for a richer sauce.

GRILLED QUAIL WITH PANCETTA AND MUSHROOMS

2 quail

1 sprig rosemary

1 slice pancetta, cut into four pieces

2 tbsp olive oil

1 garlic clove, sliced

1 tbsp finely chopped shallots

5 small portobello mushrooms, sliced (about ½ cup sliced)

1 tbsp red wine

¼ cup Homemade Chicken Stock (page 134)

Salt and freshly ground pepper as needed

Polenta (page 46)

Sautéed Spinach (recipe follows)

1. Blot the quail dry inside and out with paper toweling. Break 2 pieces from the rosemary sprig, each about 1 inch long, and set aside. Pull the needles from the remainder of the rosemary sprig and chop them (you should have about 1 teaspoon).

2. Stuff the cavity of each quail with 1 piece of rosemary and 1 piece of the pancetta. Combine the olive oil, garlic, and chopped rosemary in a 1-quart zipper-close bag. Add the quail, seal, and turn the bag a few times to coat the quail with the oil. Marinate the quail in the refrigerator for at least 4 and up to 12 hours.

3. Preheat the grill to medium heat.

4. Chop the remaining 2 pieces of pancetta and set aside.

5. Heat a small skillet over medium heat. Add the chopped pancetta and cook until lightly browned and crisp, stirring to cook evenly, 1 to 2 minutes. Transfer the pancetta to a plate with a slotted spoon. Add the shallots and sauté, stirring frequently, until tender, about 2 minutes. Add the mushrooms and cook, stirring, until golden brown, about 2 minutes. Add the wine and stir well

to dissolve any drippings. Add the chicken stock and simmer until the liquid has reduced by one-fourth, about 2 minutes. Taste and season with salt and pepper if needed.

6. Grill the quail over direct heat until cooked through and nicely browned on all sides, about 10 minutes total cooking time.

7. Spoon the polenta on to a warmed plate and top with the sautéed spinach. Nestle the quail on top of the spinach and spoon the sauce around the plate. Top with the browned pancetta bits.

SAUTÉED SPINACH

1 tsp olive oil

1 garlic clove, thinly sliced

Pinch of cracked red pepper flakes

2½ oz cleaned spinach

Salt and freshly ground pepper as needed

1. Heat the olive oil in a medium skillet over medium-low heat. Add the garlic and cook until fragrant and just starting to turn golden, about 1 minute. Add the red pepper flakes and sauté for a few seconds.

2. Add the spinach and cook, stirring as necessary, until the spinach is wilted and very hot, 2 to 3 minutes. Taste and season with salt and pepper. Serve at once.

ROAST CORNISH HEN WITH TAPENADE AND BRAISED MUSTARD GREENS

MANY OF THE ingredients in this dish can be prepped ahead of time. The tapenade can be made several days in advance or you can purchase prepared tapenade, if you are in a pinch for time. The garlic can be peeled and refrigerated. The mustard greens can be cleaned several days in advance and even blanched one day ahead.

LISA: We strongly urge you to try the greens featured in this recipe even if you think you won't like them because of their bitter flavors. Blanching the greens before sautéing them reduces the bitterness and leaves a nice spiciness that pairs well with the rest of the meal.

MARK: This recipe calls for a whole Cornish game hen, which might be more than you want at a single meal. I find it easiest to cook the entire hen, rather than splitting it while it is raw. The drippings from the hen are important to the dish since they help to give the potatoes their crispy, caramelized coating.

ROAST CORNISH GAME HEN

Tapenade (recipe follows), divided use

1¼ tsp soft butter

1 whole Cornish game hen

Salt and freshly ground pepper as needed

1 crumbled bay leaf

1 sprig oregano

1 sprig thyme

Juice of ¼ lemon

1 tsp olive oil, as needed for coating

4 oz new potatoes or fingerlings or 1 medium Yukon Gold Potato, cut into 1-inch pieces

Braised Mustard Greens (recipe follows)

1. Preheat the oven to 475°F.

2. Combine half of the tapenade with the soft butter. Rinse the Cornish hen and pat dry inside and out with paper toweling. Remove the wings at the first joint. Work your fingers underneath the skin covering the breast and carefully loosen the skin from the breast and around the legs to make a space. Stuff the tapenade mixture under the skin, spreading it evenly over the breasts and legs.

3. Season the cavity of the hen with lemon juice, salt, and pepper. Add the bay leaf, oregano, and thyme to the cavity.

4. Truss the hen with a piece of kitchen string to tie the legs close to the body. Rub the outside of the bird with the olive oil, and season it with a pinch of salt and pepper. Place the bird in a roasting pan large enough to comfortably hold both the bird and potatoes.

5. Toss potatoes with a drizzle of olive oil, and season them with a little salt and pepper. Scatter them around the hen.

6. Roast the hen until the juices run clear when you pierce the thickest part of the thigh with a skewer or kitchen fork, about 45 minutes. Baste the hen occasionally with the pan drippings and turn the potatoes once during cooking time.

7. Remove the hen from oven and set it aside to rest 5 to 10 minutes while you prepare the greens. Serve the Cornish hen and roasted potatoes on top of the mustard greens and drizzle any pan juices over the dish. Spoon the remaining tapenade around the plate.

TAPENADE

6 kalamata olives, pitted and chopped

½ anchovy filet, chopped fine

½ tsp drained, chopped capers

⅛ tsp chopped thyme

½ tsp chopped basil

½ tsp chopped parsley

Combine the olives, anchovy fillet, capers, thyme, basil, and parsley in a small bowl.

BRAISED MUSTARD GREENS

8 oz mustard greens

Salt as needed

1 tbsp olive oil

2 garlic cloves, sliced thin

¼ cup Homemade Chicken Stock (page 134)

⅛ tsp crushed red pepper

1. Trim the stems from the mustard greens and coarsely chop the leaves. Wash well and let the greens drain.

2. Bring a medium pot of water to a boil over high heat and add enough salt to season the water. Add the greens and cook until the greens are tender and wilted, about 3 minutes. Drain the greens in a colander and press on them to squeeze out as much water as possible.

3. Return the pot to medium heat and add the olive oil. When the oil is warm but not smoking, add the garlic slices and cook, stirring frequently, until golden, about 1 minute. Add the chicken stock, red pepper, and mustard greens. Increase the heat to medium-high and cook until the greens are heated through and most of the liquid cooks away, 1 or 2 minutes. Season with salt and serve.

sausage and fig skewers two ways
with sautéed swiss chard and chickpeas

SOME SMALLER MARKETS may offer individual sausage links, ideal when you only need a small amount. If you have to buy a larger quantity, freeze what you don't need or add it to a pasta dish like Penne with Broccoli Rabe and Garlic (page 113) or Rigatoni with Sausage, Bacon, and Onions (page 114), or sauté it to serve with the chicken in the Chicken with Apples and Prunes (page 122).

MARK: I gravitate toward Spain when I make this dish. Manchego cheese is made with sheep's milk and has a rich, rustic flavor that is a perfect accompaniment to the chorizo in my version of the dish.

LISA: Italian sausage is my favorite for this dish, and I change the glaze ingredients slightly for a more Italian flavor. Pecorino Toscano is my choice here for its nutty flavor which stands up well to the sausage. This cheese can usually be found in a store with a fine cheese selection.

LISA'S VERSION

GLAZE

1 tsp extra-virgin olive oil

1 tbsp balsamic vinegar

2 tsp honey

1 tsp soy sauce

4 oz hot or sweet Italian sausage, cut into 1-inch-thick rounds

4 whole fresh or dried figs, halved (see Note)

Sautéed Swiss Chard and Chickpeas (recipe follows)

Grilled country-style bread (page 143)

Pecorino Toscano cheese, cut in thin slices

Lemon wedge

1. Preheat a grill to medium (page 144). If you are using a gas grill, leave one burner off; if you are using charcoal, push the coals to one side to create a spot for indirect cooking.

2. Whisk together the glaze ingredients in a small dish and set aside.

3. Thread the sausage rounds alternating them with fig halves on 1 or 2 skewers. Grill the skewers over indirect heat, turning and brushing with glaze occasionally until the sausage is browned and cooked through, about 10 minutes total cooking time.

4. Place the chard in the center of a plate. Lay sausage and figs on top, and serve with grilled bread, pecorino cheese, and a lemon wedge.

PREPARING FRESH AND DRIED FIGS

When fresh figs are in season we enjoy them in as many ways as possible. For this dish you need only to rinse the fresh figs and cut them in half lengthwise.

Dried figs need to be reconstituted first. Put the figs in a small bowl and add a tablespoon of a dry white or red wine and 2 tablespoons of water. Heat the figs in the microwave until they are softened, 1 or 1½ minutes.

MARK'S VERSION

GLAZE

2 tsp extra-virgin olive oil

2 tsp sherry vinegar

2 tsp honey

¼ tsp anchovy paste

4 whole fresh or dried figs, stemmed and halved

4 oz Spanish-style chorizo sausage

Sautéed Swiss Chard and Chickpeas (recipe follows)

Grilled country-style bread (page 143)

Manchego cheese, cut in thin slices

Lemon wedge

1. Preheat a grill to medium (page 144). If you are using a gas grill, leave one burner off; if you are using charcoal, push the coals to one side to create a spot for indirect cooking.

2. Whisk together the glaze ingredients in a small dish and set aside.

3. Thread the sausage rounds alternating with fig halves on 1 or 2 skewers. Grill the skewers over indirect heat, turning and brushing with glaze occasionally until the sausage is browned and cooked through, about 7 minutes.

4. Place the chard in the center of a plate. Lay the sausage and figs on top and serve with grilled bread, Manchego cheese, and a lemon wedge.

SAUTÉED SWISS CHARD AND CHICKPEAS

4 oz Swiss chard

2 tsp olive oil

1 large clove garlic, sliced thin

⅓ cup cooked chickpeas (page 136)

1 tbsp water or Homemade Chicken Stock (page 134)

Crushed red pepper flakes to taste

Salt and freshly ground pepper as needed

1. Trim the stems from the Swiss chard and chop the leaves. Rinse well and let the chard drain in a colander.

2. Heat the olive oil in a sauté pan over medium-low heat. When the oil is hot, add the garlic slices and cook, stirring frequently, until golden, about 1 minute. Add the chard, chickpeas, water or chicken stock, and red pepper flakes. Simmer, stirring occasionally, until the chard is tender, about 4 minutes. Season with salt and pepper.

short ribs braised in stout with roasted vegetables

LISA: Short ribs are a favorite meal in our family. Cooked until tender, they're always moist, juicy, and rich in flavor. The roasted vegetables are quick and easy; you can make them while the short ribs are braising.

MARK: Because braising requires a large amount of liquid to keep the meat moist while cooking, we've included enough meat in this recipe to make two portions. You can eat half now and freeze some for another time. Freeze any extra sauce from the braise in small quantities to use in a pan sauce.

MAKES 2 PORTIONS

½ tsp canola oil

Salt and freshly ground pepper as needed

2 lb beef short ribs

Flour for dusting

½ onion, diced

1 garlic clove, minced

1½ tsp tomato paste

2 cups Homemade Chicken Stock (page 134)

½ bottle stout or dark beer or ¾ cup dry red wine

1 small bay leaf

2 sprigs fresh thyme

1 small sprig rosemary

Roasted Vegetables (recipe follows)

1. Preheat the oven to 325°F.

2. Heat a medium Dutch oven with oil over medium heat. Salt and pepper the ribs, and then coat them lightly with flour, shaking off any excess. Add the ribs to the pot and cook until well browned on all sides, about 6 minutes total. Remove the ribs to a plate and set aside.

3. Pour most of the oil from the pot, leaving about ½ teaspoon (enough to coat the pan). Add the onion and garlic and turn the heat to low. Cook, stirring frequently, until golden brown, 3 to 4 minutes. Add the tomato paste and cook, still stirring frequently, until it turns brick red, about 1 minute. Add the stock, beer, and herbs; stir to blend the mixture. Return the ribs to pot, increase the heat to medium-high, cover the Dutch oven, and bring the stock to a boil.

4. Immediately place the Dutch oven in the oven. Braise until the short ribs are very tender when pierced with a fork and the meat falls easily from the bones, about 2 hours. The meat should remain at a slow simmer while cooking. Adjust the oven temperature if necessary.

5. Transfer the short ribs to a platter and put the Dutch oven with the sauce on the stove top over high heat. Bring the sauce to a boil and skim the fat from surface. Reduce

the sauce until it is flavorful and thickened enough to lightly coat a spoon, 8 to 10 minutes. Remove and discard the thyme and rosemary. If you like, purée the sauce in the food processor for a thicker consistency. Season the sauce with salt and pepper to taste.

6. Serve the short ribs with the sauce, accompanied by roasted vegetables.

ROASTED VEGETABLES

2½ cups cubed root vegetables (carrots, parsnips, rutabaga, potato, sweet potato, and/or onion, about 1-inch cubes)

1 tbsp olive oil

2 or 3 thyme sprigs

Salt and freshly ground pepper as needed

1. Preheat the oven to 425°F.

2. On a nonstick baking sheet, toss the vegetables with the oil, thyme, salt, and pepper. Roast on the bottom rack of oven, turning once until browned and tender, about 25 minutes. Serve hot.

blackberry barbecued pork tenderloin with sweet potato salad

LISA: This menu was inspired by the bounty of the South. Sweet potatoes are a perfect companion to the pork. In addition to being delicious and flavorful, they have a great color. Bright colors translate into healthy foods. The salad is generous in size, as it does not make sense to cook half of a sweet potato, but leftovers are delicious the next day.

MARK: The Blackberry Barbecue Sauce can be made ahead and stored in the refrigerator for several weeks or frozen for 2 months. The recipe makes enough to glaze one whole pork tenderloin. Since you usually have to buy the whole tenderloin, I generally divide the sauce and the pork in two, prepare half, and store the rest in the freezer to cook another time. The glaze also goes well with chicken.

BLACKBERRY BARBECUED PORK TENDERLOIN

½ pork tenderloin (6 to 8 oz), trimmed

Salt and freshly ground pepper as needed

3 tbsp Blackberry Barbecue Sauce (recipe follows)

1. Heat the grill to medium heat. Season the pork tenderloin with salt and pepper and grill over direct heat until browned on all sides. Move to indirect heat and continue cooking and turning often while basting with the barbecue sauce, about 15 to 20 minutes. Be careful not to burn the glaze.

2. Set the pork aside to rest for 10 minutes before slicing. Serve the sliced pork drizzled with a little more of the barbecue sauce accompanied by the sweet potato salad.

BLACKBERRY BARBECUE SAUCE

MAKES ⅓ CUP, ENOUGH FOR ONE WHOLE TENDERLOIN

½ cup blackberries

2 tbsp cider vinegar

2 tbsp water

3 tbsp brown sugar

⅛ tsp ground cloves

¼ tsp grated fresh ginger

½ tsp ground cinnamon

Pinch cayenne pepper

Salt as needed

1 tsp butter

1. Mash the blackberries with the back of a wooden spoon in a small saucepot. Add the vinegar, water, brown sugar, and spices. Continue to mash and stir well.

2. Bring the sauce to a boil over medium-high heat. Reduce the heat to low and continue to simmer until the sauce is thickened, about 10 minutes.

3. Remove the pan from the heat and whisk in the butter.

4. Strain the sauce through a fine mesh sieve into a bowl, pressing the blackberries with the back of a spoon to extract as much flavor as possible without forcing the seeds into the sauce.

SWEET POTATO SALAD

DRESSING

3 tbsp olive oil

1 tsp ketchup

1 tsp Dijon-style mustard

1 tsp red wine vinegar

1 tsp lemon juice

½ tsp minced garlic

½ to 1 tsp finely chopped jalapeño pepper, to taste

6 oz sweet potato (1 average), cut into medium dice

½ cup small-diced red and/or green pepper

¼ cup minced red onion, soaked in ice water for 15 minutes and drained

4 tsp minced cilantro

1. Whisk together the dressing ingredients.

2. Put the sweet potatoes in a small saucepot and add enough cold water to cover them. Add enough salt to season the water.

3. Bring the water a boil over medium-high heat, and then reduce the heat to low. Simmer the potatoes until they are just tender to the bite, about 10 minutes.

4. Drain the sweet potatoes in a colander and rinse under running cold water to cool them. Blot them dry on paper towels.

5. Combine the sweet potatoes, pepper, onion, and half of the cilantro in a salad bowl. Pour the dressing over everything and toss gently to avoid mashing the sweet potatoes. Taste and season with salt and pepper. Sprinkle the salad with remaining cilantro.

baked apple with oatmeal crunch

MARK: For this dessert, we chose apple varieties that hold their shape during cooking, but you can certainly go with your own preference. Bear in mind that different apple varieties have different baking times.

LISA: This is the perfect fall dessert. The oatmeal crunch elevates this simple fruit to "indulgent dessert" status. I usually double the recipe for a satisfying breakfast the next morning, either eaten cold or quickly reheated in the microwave.

1 baking apple, such as Honeycrisp or Golden Delicious

1 tbsp walnut pieces

2 tsp dried tart cherries or raisins

¼ tsp cinnamon

1 tsp brown sugar

Pinch orange zest

2 tsp rolled oats

½ tsp unsalted butter

½ cup apple cider or orange juice

Greek yogurt, optional

1. Preheat the oven to 375°F.

2. To prepare the apple, peel the skin off the top third. Use a small melon baller to scoop out the stem and core and to make a shallow 2-inch wide crater in the top of apple to hold the oatmeal topping. Stand the apple upright in a small individual gratin or baking dish.

3. Mix the walnuts, cherries, cinnamon, brown sugar, and zest together in a small bowl. Stuff the apple with half of the nut mixture, using all of the cherries.

4. Add the oatmeal and butter to the remaining nut mixture. Use your fingertips to work in the butter until the mixture is crumbly and just barely holds together when squeezed lightly. Spoon this over the filling, patting it onto the crater-like top of the apple to seal in the filling.

5. Pour the cider or juice into the gratin or baking dish and cover loosely with foil. Bake the apple until it is nearly tender, about 30 minutes. Uncover the apple and continue to bake until it is tender when pierced with a knife and the oatmeal is browned and crisp, about 20 more minutes. Baste the top once and baste the sides of apple frequently with the juices in the baking dish.

6. Serve the baked apple warm, at room temperature, or cold. It can be topped with a dollop of Greek yogurt for added creaminess, if you like.

PEAR BREAD PUDDING

MARK: This is just the beginning of a versatile dessert/breakfast we think you will want to make again and again. The variations of fruits and spices are endless; you can try something different every time. Consider these replacements or combinations:

- Star anise instead of cinnamon; the licorice flavor marries well with pears.

- White loaf bread, challah, brioche or cinnamon bread instead of French bread listed in the recipe. (This is the perfect dish for using up stale bread.)

- Framboise if you are using raspberries.

- Freshly grated nutmeg, cinnamon, and ginger to season sautéed apples and a splash of Calvados instead of vanilla in the custard.

- Peaches or plums sautéed with a piece of vanilla bean and a bit of lemon or orange zest.

LISA: This dessert is truly indulgent when made with half-and-half or cream, resulting in a silky and rich custard. At the other extreme, I've also used just skim milk to lower the calories and it is still good, plus I don't feel guilty about enjoying dessert on a weeknight. Any leftovers are terrific warmed in the microwave and eaten for breakfast the next morning.

½ tsp butter

1 small pear, peeled, quartered, cored and cut into 1½-inch pieces

1 small piece cinnamon stick (about 1 inch), or ½ whole star anise

10 dried tart cherries or raisins

1 egg yolk

½ cup half-and-half (or cream, milk, or a combination)

2 tbsp sugar

1 tsp vanilla

Two ½-inch-thick slices French bread, cut into cubes

Cinnamon sugar: ¼ tsp granulated sugar and ⅛ tsp cinnamon mixed together

1. Preheat the oven to 350°F.

2. Heat the butter in a small sauté pan over medium-low heat. Add the pears and cinnamon stick and sauté until tender, about 5 minutes. Add the cherries, remove from the heat, and spoon into the bottom of a small buttered gratin or baking dish.

3. Whisk the egg yolk, half-and-half, sugar, and vanilla together in a small bowl. Add the bread cubes and stir. Pour this mixture over the pears and let the pudding rest for 20 minutes, occasionally pressing down on the bread to keep it as submerged as possible.

4. Sprinkle the pudding with cinnamon sugar and set the dish in a hot water bath. Bake until the pudding is puffed, browned, and set, 50 to 60 minutes. Serve warm or at room temperature.

spiced fall fruits with orange flower water and yogurt

THIS COMPOTE OF seasonal fruits makes for a quick dessert. If you decide to make extra, it can be a perfect breakfast dish by increasing the nuts to give it more sustenance.

LISA: Compotes are easy to make and work with many fruits. Vary the syrup according to the season and the fruit, such as star anise with dried fruits, pears, and nuts.

MARK: Orange flower water can be found in many specialty stores in the spice and flavoring section. It is also a staple in Middle Eastern markets. Its flavor and aroma add depth to a dish. We suggest it in the cookie recipe (page 133) and the apricot pudding souffle (page 27). It pairs well with strawberries, apricots or peaches tossed with sugar. Another simple dessert would be fresh figs, on a plate with a scoop of ricotta cheese mixed with a touch of orange flower water, drizzled with honey, and sprinkled with pistachios or toasted walnuts. Like other fragrant flavors, a little goes a long way.

¾ cup assorted fruits, such as halved figs, wedges of pears, prune plums, or apples; grapes, cranberries, raspberries, dried fruits

SYRUP

1 tbsp honey

2 tbsp water

2 tbsp orange juice

2 tbsp white wine

¼ cinnamon stick

¼ vanilla bean, split and scraped

1 whole clove

1½ inch piece orange rind, pith removed

¼ tsp orange flower water

GARNISH

Greek yogurt

Toasted chopped walnuts or pine nuts

1. Preheat the oven to 350°F.
2. Place the prepared fruits, with the exception of soft berries, in a small individual gratin dish.
3. Combine all of the syrup ingredients in a small saucepan. Bring to a boil, reduce the heat, and simmer very low for 5 minutes. Remove from the heat and pour the syrup over the fruits.
4. Bake for 15 minutes, basting occasionally. Remove from the oven, and add any soft berries if you are using them. Drizzle with orange flower water, and stir carefully to combine.
5. Serve warm or at room temperature with a spoonful of Greek yogurt and a sprinkling of nuts.

fig and raspberry gratin with honey lavender semifreddo

LISA: Lavender blossoms can be purchased dry in specialty markets, and are available in fresh bunches at some farmers' markets. I use lavender all summer in shortbread cookies, poaching syrups for fruit, and I particularly like it in iced tea. I steep a sprig with the teabags and boiling water. (Fair warning, though, a little goes a long way!)

HONEY LAVENDER SEMIFREDDO

THE SEMIFREDDO RECIPE keeps in the freezer for several days, ideal if you need something that can be made ahead of time.

¼ cup heavy cream

¼ tsp lavender blossoms, untreated

1 egg yolk

2 tbsp honey

1. Using a small saucepan or in a microwaveable bowl, bring the cream to a boil. Remove from the heat. Add the lavender, cover, and steep for 15 minutes. Strain, reserve 1½ tablespoons of cream, and put the remainder in a small bowl in the refrigerator to chill until very cold.

2. Whisk the egg yolk, honey, and reserved 1½ tablespoons of cream in a medium metal bowl. Place it over a small saucepan of simmering water (the bottom of the bowl should not touch the water). Whisk constantly until very thick and completely emulsified, about 4 minutes. Remove the bowl from the water and continue whisking until cool and thick, about 3 to 4 minutes.

3. Whisk the remaining chilled lavender cream in a small bowl to soft peaks. Using a spatula, fold a bit of cream into the yolk mixture to lighten it. Carefully fold in the rest of the cream. Cover and freeze until firm. Semifreddos do not freeze as hard as ice cream and maintain a silky texture.

FIG AND RASPBERRY GRATIN

THIS GRATIN CAN be made with any variety of fruits that are in season. Plums and peaches are another good match for the semifreddo..

2 figs, stemmed and halved

1 tbsp red wine

1½ tsp brown sugar

¼ cup raspberries

Toasted walnuts or pine nuts, to taste

1. Preheat the oven to 425°F.

2. Place the figs in a small gratin dish. Drizzle with wine and sprinkle with brown sugar. Bake for 15 minutes, basting once. Scatter the raspberries around the figs, baste again. Bake 5 more minutes.

3. Serve the gratin warm, topped with a scoop of the semifreddo and a sprinkling of toasted nuts.

CHAPTER FOUR

Winter

the winter pantry

Winter is a quiet time for produce. Many of our favorite fruits and vegetables of this season come from cold storage or root cellars. Although the offerings aren't as numerous as for summer and fall, there's still a lot to like about the foods of winter.

VEGETABLES		FRUITS
Artichokes	Horseradish	Apples
Beets	Jerusalem artichoke	Bananas
Bok choy	Kohlrabi	Pears
Broccoli	Leeks	Blood oranges
Brussels sprouts	Lettuces	Persimmons
Cabbage	Mushrooms	Clementines
Cardoon	Onions	Pomegranates
Carrots	Parsnips	Cranberries
Celeriac	Potatoes	Pummelos
Celery	Rutabagas	Grapefruit
Daikon	Shallots	Kiwi
Garlic	Sweet potatoes	Satsuma oranges
Greens such as spinach, arugula,	Turnips	Kumquats
kale, Swiss chard, collards	Winter squash and pumpkin	Passion fruit
		Tangerines

chicken paprikas soup

HUNGARIAN CHICKEN PAPRIKAS is one of our favorites, but this version, made as a soup, is lighter and quicker to prepare, and still contains all of the flavors we love. If you have some cooked noodles already on hand, you have saved yourself a step. Put them in your soup bowl and heat them in the microwave before you ladle the soup on top. The soup keeps for up to 3 days in the refrigerator. If you want to make this soup ahead of time, keep the soup and the noodles separate until you are ready to eat.

½ tsp caraway seeds

3 oz boneless skinless chicken breast

1 tsp canola oil, divided use

½ cup diced onion

3 mushrooms, halved and sliced thin

1 tsp minced garlic

1 tsp sweet paprika

1½ cups Homemade Chicken Stock (page 134)

¾ oz egg noodles

1 tsp chopped parsley, optional

Sour cream or plain Greek-style yogurt, to taste

1. Warm a small sauté pan over medium-high heat. Add the caraway seeds and cook, stirring or swirling the pan constantly, until the seeds are fragrant and toasted, about 1 minute. Pound them to a fine grind in a mortar and pestle. Set aside.

2. Cut the chicken breast crosswise into thin bite-size strips. Heat ½ teaspoon of the oil in a small pot over medium heat. Add the chicken pieces and sauté, stirring from time to time, until the chicken is just cooked through but not browned, 4 to 5 minutes. Transfer to a small plate and set aside.

3. Heat the remaining ½ teaspoon of oil in the same pan over medium heat. Add the onion, mushrooms, and garlic and sauté, stirring frequently, until the onion is starting to turn golden, about 3 minutes. Add the paprika, ground caraway, and stock; bring to a boil. Reduce the heat to low and simmer until the flavors are blended, about 10 minutes.

4. While soup is simmering, cook the egg noodles separately in boiling salted water until tender (follow the package directions). Drain the noodles in a colander and transfer to a heated soup bowl.

5. Add the chicken breast to the soup and heat thoroughly, about 1 minute. Spoon the soup over the noodles, sprinkle with the chopped parsley, if using, and top with a dollop of sour cream or yogurt.

asian noodle soup

LISA: We returned from a culinary trip to Vietnam several years ago with a great fondness for the food. Every dish had such remarkable, fresh flavors. That trip has influenced both my culinary imagination and my cooking style. Vietnamese dishes are bright and light because the cooks use the freshest foods and add intense bursts of flavor both in the dish and as an accompaniment: raw onions, fresh lime, cilantro, and chiles.

MARK: This is a good mulligan meal. You can add leftover meats, seafood, and fish instead of, or in addition to, the shrimp. Shrimp and pork are a traditional combination. The vegetables can be varied as well. Think about the colors and textures that might add to the appeal of this soup: spinach, mushrooms, red pepper, and thinly sliced carrots are all possibilities.

For a soup like this one, we suggest making your own stock. The delicate flavors are at their best with the fresh clean taste of homemade chicken stock.

2 oz rice vermicelli sticks

½ tsp vegetable or stir-fry oil

½ tsp minced garlic

¼ lb shrimp, peeled and deveined

4 cherry tomatoes, quartered

1¼ cups Homemade Chicken Stock (page 134)

2 tsp fish sauce (nuoc nam)

6 snow peas or sugar snaps, stringed and halved

1½ cups sliced bok choy (sliced on an angle into 2-inch-long pieces)

Soy sauce to taste

2 scallions, sliced thin (white and green portions)

2 thin slices red onion

GARNISHES

2 oz bean sprouts

6 paper-thin slices serrano or jalapeño chile

1 lime wedge

2 tbsp whole cilantro leaves

1. Bring a large pot of water to a boil over high heat. Add the noodles and stir to separate the strands. Return to a boil and cook until softened and white but still resilient, 4 to 5 minutes. Drain the noodles in a colander, rinse them with cold water to halt the cooking, and set them aside to drain at room temperature.

2. Heat the oil in a small saucepot or wok over moderate heat. Add the garlic and sauté, stirring constantly, until it is fragrant, about 5 seconds. Add the shrimp and tomatoes; stir-fry until the shrimp is just pink, 2 to 3 minutes.

3. Add the stock and the fish sauce, increase the heat to high, and bring the stock to a boil. Add the snow peas and bok choy, and return the stock to a boil, continuing to cook another 45 to 60 seconds. Season to taste with soy sauce. Stir in the scallions and onion slices.

4. Place the rice noodles in the middle of a large soup bowl and ladle the soup over noodles. Top with the garnishes.

The variety of noodles in an authentic Asian market is vast and can be daunting. Look for bags that say one of the following: bun, rice sticks or rice vermicelli.

MIDDLE EASTERN CARROTS

THIS IS A slightly more exotic version of traditional glazed carrots. The recipe is quite versatile and would go well with anything from Middle Eastern lamb and couscous to a traditional American turkey dinner.

2 medium carrots

⅛ cup water

⅛ cup orange juice

1-inch piece cinnamon stick

½ tsp unsalted butter

½ tsp honey

1 rounded tsp currants

Salt and pepper as needed

⅛ tsp grated ginger

⅛ tsp grated orange zest

1. Peel the carrots and cut them crosswise on a diagonal into ½-inch-long pieces. Place the carrots in a small sauté pan with the water, juice, cinnamon, butter, honey, currants, salt, and pepper. Bring to a boil over medium heat. Cover the pan, reduce the heat to low, and simmer, until the carrots are tender, about 8 minutes. Remove and discard the cinnamon.

2. Uncover the pan and continue to simmer until the liquid is reduced to a glaze that clings to the carrots, another 2 minutes. Be careful that the liquid does not evaporate completely or start to burn. Add a few drops more water if necessary.

3. Add the ginger and orange zest off the heat. Taste and season with salt and pepper. Serve hot.

mushroom, leek, fontina, and truffle oil pizza

THIS ELEGANT PIZZA reflects the rich flavors of winter's bounty—sautéed mushrooms and leeks topped with creamy Fontina cheese. The truffle oil is optional, but if you have a small bottle, this is the time to use it.

2 tsp olive oil

1 small leek, halved lengthwise and sliced crosswise into ¼ inch ribbons (white and light green portions only)

2 oz sliced mushrooms

½ tsp chopped thyme

½ tsp minced garlic

Salt and freshly ground pepper as needed

One 6-oz ball Pizza Dough (page 142)

Flour for rolling dough

Cornmeal for dusting peel

Olive oil for brushing dough

¼ to ⅓ cup grated Fontina cheese

4 or 5 drops truffle oil (optional)

1. Place a pizza stone on the bottom rack in the oven. Dust a pizza peel (or a baking sheet with no sides) with cornmeal and set aside. Preheat the oven to 500°F, allowing at least 30 minutes for the pizza stone to heat thoroughly.

2. Heat the olive oil in a small skillet over medium heat. Add the leek and stir to coat with the oil. Cover the skillet and cook the leek over low heat until tender, about 5 minutes. Add the mushrooms, thyme, and garlic. Cook, uncovered, stirring occasionally, until the mushrooms are tender and lightly browned, about 3 minutes. Season with salt and pepper.

3. Roll out the dough on floured surface or stretch it into an 8-inch circle.

4. Scatter a little cornmeal on a pizza peel (or use a baking sheet that does not have sides). Transfer the dough to the pizza peel and brush the dough with just enough olive oil to lightly coat the surface.

5. Spoon the leek and mushroom mixture over the pizza, leaving a ¾-inch border. Slide the pizza from the peel to the pizza stone and bake until the edges are browned, about 10 minutes.

6. Sprinkle the Fontina cheese over the top and continue to bake until the cheese is melted, another 1 or 2 minutes. Drizzle the truffle oil over the pizza, if using, cut it into slices, and serve hot.

penne with broccoli rabe, olive oil, and garlic

LISA: I have served this family favorite at our house for many years. It is a quick dish to make and even easier if the vegetables are prepped earlier in the week. For this dish, peel the garlic and refrigerate it whole. The broccoli rabe can be cut, washed, spun dry, and stored in the refrigerator several days in advance. Broccoli rabe is often sold in small bunches, but if you have more than you need for this dish, have it another night, blanched first, and then sautéed in olive oil with lots of garlic and a few red pepper flakes. Finish the sauté with a squeeze of fresh lemon juice.

MARK: I like to add some sausage to the recipe. To do that, I slice or crumble the sausage and sauté it in the olive oil over medium heat until it is cooked through before adding the garlic in step 3.

4 oz broccoli rabe

3 oz penne pasta

1½ tbsp olive oil

1 tbsp minced garlic

¼ tsp crushed red pepper

Salt and freshly ground pepper as needed

Freshly grated Parmesan

1. To prepare the broccoli rabe, cut off the ends, and then cut it crosswise into 1½-inch-wide pieces. Wash the broccoli rabe in cold water and allow it to drain in a colander.

2. Bring a medium pot of cold water to boil over high heat and add enough salt to season the water. Add the pasta, stir to separate, and cook according to the package directions.

3. While the pasta is cooking, heat a skillet with the olive oil over low heat. Add the garlic and crushed red pepper. Cook very slowly, stirring frequently, until the garlic is just starting to turn golden, about 3 minutes. Remove the skillet from the heat and set aside.

4. Add the broccoli rabe to the pasta 1 minute before the pasta is fully cooked (use the cooking time on the package as a guide). Stir to completely submerge the broccoli rabe and cook until the pasta is al dente and the broccoli rabe is bright green, about 1 minute. Ladle out 2 or 3 tablespoons of the pasta water and reserve to finish the sauce. Drain the pasta and broccoli rabe in a colander.

5. Return the skillet to medium heat and add the broccoli rabe and pasta, tossing the ingredients together. Season with a little salt and pepper. Add the reserved pasta water a little at a time until the pasta is moistened. Serve in a pasta bowl with topped with some of the grated Parmesan.

rigatoni with sausage, bacon, and onions

THE SAUCE FOR the rigatoni makes enough to serve two, so either double up the pasta and invite a friend to share your table, or pack the extra sauce away in the refrigerator or freezer. It also makes a great topping for pizza or grilled polenta. Small grocery stores with butcher counters often sell individual sausages and bacon slices, so you can buy only as much as you need for a recipe. We've included a recipe for a large batch of tomato sauce (page 135) but feel free to use any tomato sauce you like in this recipe.

½ medium onion

3 oz bacon (2 strips)

1 link hot or sweet fresh Italian sausage (6 oz)

2 tbsp dry red wine

1¾ cups tomato sauce (page 135)

3 oz rigatoni pasta (or 6 oz to serve 2)

Grated Parmesan cheese as needed

1. Cut the onion into thirds lengthwise and then thinly slice it crosswise. Cut the bacon crosswise into ⅓-inch-wide pieces. Cut the sausage in half lengthwise, then cut the halves crosswise at an angle into 1-inch-thick pieces.

2. Heat a sauté pan over medium heat. Add the onion and bacon and cook, stirring occasionally, until the onion and bacon are browned, about 10 minutes. Pour the mixture into a colander to let it drain.

3. Return the pan to the stove and add the sausage. Cook, turning the pieces as necessary, until browned on all sides, about 3 minutes. Add the sausage to the colander holding the bacon and onion. Toss briefly to combine, blot lightly with paper toweling, and set aside.

4. Return the pan to medium heat, add the red wine, and stir well to release any drippings. Let the wine reduce by one-fourth, about 2 minutes. Add the tomato sauce and bring it to boil. Reduce the heat to low and add the onion, bacon, and sausage mixture. Cover the pan and simmer the sauce over low heat until flavorful, 15 to 20 minutes.

5. Cook the rigatoni in salted boiling water according to directions on package. Drain the pasta in a colander, shaking it to get rid of the excess water. Add enough of the sauce to dress the pasta and toss to combine. Spoon the pasta into a warmed bowl and serve with grated Parmesan cheese.

black bean chili

MARK: Dried chipotle pepper flakes can be found in the spice section of the grocery store. Unlike canned chipotle peppers, which have to be refrigerated once you open them, this form stores well in the pantry for a long period of time, even after it is opened. We use it to add a bit of smoke and heat to a dish.

LISA: Canned tomatoes give this chili a richer flavor than the lackluster fresh tomatoes you typically find in the winter months. This recipe uses about half of one can. You can freeze the leftover canned diced tomatoes to be used later in another recipe.

½ tsp olive oil

¼ cup minced onion

1 tsp minced garlic

2 tbsp small-dice red pepper

1½ tsp chili powder

½ tsp ground cumin

¼ tsp dried oregano

Pinch chipotle pepper flakes, optional

¾ cup canned diced tomatoes

1 cup cooked black beans (page 136)

¼ cup water

Salt as needed

Lime juice as needed

GARNISHES

Cilantro leaves

Chopped scallions

Chopped jalapeño pepper

Sour cream

1. Heat the olive oil in a small pot over medium heat. Add the onion, reduce the heat to low, and sauté until the onion is tender and translucent, about 5 minutes.

2. Add the garlic, pepper, chili powder, cumin, oregano, and chipotle, if using. Stir to combine and cook until the garlic is fragrant, another 2 minutes.

3. Add the tomatoes, beans, and water and bring to a simmer. Cover the pot and simmer very slowly until the chili is flavorful and all of the ingredients are tender, about 45 minutes. Taste and season with salt and lime juice.

4. Serve the chili in a bowl topped with the garnishes.

Canned black beans can be substituted. Add the canned beans during the last 20 minutes of cooking. Chili freezes well, so this can be made ahead or double the portion and freeze half for another day.

braised gigante beans

LISA: This traditional Greek recipe is delicious and versatile. It is a perfect side dish for grilled or roasted lamb and poultry, and can also become the main course when served with a sautéed green vegetable, such as spinach or broccoli rabe. In Greece, it is often served at room temperature and featured as part of a meze (small plates of hors d'oeuvres).

MARK: This recipe does require some advance preparation, but you can break the work up into stages to suit your schedule. The beans need to soak overnight. The next day, simmer them until tender and let them cool right in the cooking liquid. They'll last for 2 or 3 days. Bake them with the tomatoes another day. Once the dish is completed, you can keep it refrigerated for 3 or 4 days, or you can freeze it for several weeks.

½ lb gigante beans, also known as giant limas or corona beans

1½ tbsp olive oil

1½ cups diced onion

1½ tsp minced garlic

1 tbsp honey

1½ tbsp diced oven-dried or sun-dried tomatoes

1 cup canned diced tomatoes, preferably fire-roasted

1 bay leaf

2 sprigs oregano

1 tbsp red wine vinegar

Salt and freshly ground pepper as needed

1. Rinse the beans and place them in a bowl. Add enough cold water to cover them by a couple of inches. Place the bowl in the refrigerator and soak the beans at least 8 and up to 12 hours.

2. Drain the beans and place them in a pot. Add enough water to cover them by 2 inches. Put the pot over medium-high heat and bring to a boil, skimming any foam that rises to the surface. Turn the heat down to low and simmer the beans very gently, skimming as necessary, until the beans are just starting to be tender to the bite, about 1 hour. Remove the pot from the heat and let the beans rest in the water. (The beans can be refrigerated at this point and the recipe completed the next day.)

3. Preheat the oven to 300°F.

4. Heat the olive oil in a large Dutch oven over low heat. Add the onion and garlic and sauté, stirring frequently, until tender and translucent, about 10 minutes. Add the honey, diced oven-dried and canned tomatoes, bay leaf, and oregano; stir well.

5. Transfer the beans to the Dutch oven using a slotted spoon to scoop them out of their cooking liquid. Use a slotted spoon to scoop the beans out of the cooking liquid and transfer them to the Dutch oven. Add 2 cups of the cooking liquid and bring to a boil over medium-high heat.

6. Cover, place in the oven, and braise the beans until they are tender and the liq-

uid has thickened, about 3 hours. Check the beans as they cook to make sure that the liquid stays at a low simmer, adjusting the oven temperature as necessary.

7. Taste the beans and season them with vinegar, salt, and pepper. Serve hot or at room temperature.

SAUTÉED BRUSSELS SPROUTS WITH PECANS

THE BRUSSELS SPROUTS in this recipe taste like an entirely different vegetable from the boiled ones we grew up with. Quickly sautéing them retains their crisp yet tender texture and delicate flavor. Surprisingly enough, we have found that even children will eat these. If you think you do not like Brussels sprouts, try this version and we believe that you, too, will become a convert. Toasted walnuts, hazelnuts or pine nuts can be substituted for the pecans in this recipe. Some stores sell toasted nuts which saves a step in the preparation process. Brussels sprouts can be peeled and sliced a day ahead if desired.

5 or 6 Brussels sprouts

½ tsp butter

1½ tbsp finely diced onion

Salt and freshly ground pepper as needed

2 tbsp water

1½ tsp coarsely chopped toasted pecans

1. Trim the stem ends of the Brussels sprouts and use the tip of a paring knife to cut out the core. Carefully peel off as many whole leaves as possible. Cut the remaining tightly bound inner leaves into very thin slices.

2. Heat the butter in small sauté pan over medium heat. Add the onion and sauté until translucent. Add the Brussels sprouts, season with salt and pepper, and toss to combine. Add the water. Bring to a boil, cover the pan, and cook until tender, 3 to 4 minutes. Be careful to prevent them from browning too much, although a little bit of caramelization is fine.

3. Uncover and cook until all of the water is evaporated. Add the pecans and adjust the seasoning to taste. Serve hot.

grilled pancetta-wrapped shrimp with meyer lemon relish

LISA: Meyer lemons, once rarely seen outside of California, are now available in many markets during the winter months. A Meyer lemon is not as tart as a regular lemon, with a floral scent and a sweet flavor. If you cannot get Niçoise olives, any mild flavored variety can be substituted. The olive bar or salad bar in your grocery store is a good source when you need to buy a small amount.

MARK: Pancetta, as well as proscuitto, can usually be purchased by the slice in the deli department, but if you buy a whole package of pre-sliced meat, you can freeze the leftovers as long as the slices are separated with paper, which is usually the way it is packaged. You'll find it very convenient to grab a slice to add to pizza or pasta dishes. The slices thaw in a few minutes sitting on the counter.

PANCETTA-WRAPPED SHRIMP

6 large shrimp (about 5 oz)

3 slices pancetta

2 to 3 cups mixed winter salad greens (e.g., radicchio, watercress, frisée, chervil, oak leaf)

2 tsp extra-virgin olive oil

Salt and freshly ground pepper as needed

Meyer Lemon Relish (recipe follows)

1. Preheat a grill or broiler to medium.
2. Peel and devein the shrimp, but leave the "tail intact. Cut the pancetta in half and wrap one piece around each shrimp, securing the pancetta on the shrimp with a toothpick.

3. Grill the shrimp over medium heat on the first side until the pancetta is crisp and the shrimp starts to turn bright pink, about 2 minutes. Turn once and finish grilling on the second side, another 2 minutes. Alternatively, the shrimp can be prepared indoors, sautéed, broiled, or cooked on a stove top grill.

4. Toss the salad greens with olive oil and season with salt and pepper. Mound the greens on a plate. Remove the toothpicks from the shrimp and place them around the salad. Spoon a bit of relish over each shrimp. Serve any remaining relish on the side.

MEYER LEMON RELISH

THIS RELISH USES an entire Meyer lemon, peel and all. If you substitute a regular variety of lemon, remove the peel before proceeding with the recipe.

½ whole Meyer lemon

2 tsp finely diced shallots

5 Niçoise olives, pitted and cut into thin slivers

1 tsp chopped basil

1 tsp chopped parsley

1 tsp extra-virgin olive oil

Pinch crushed red pepper flakes

Salt as needed

1. Cut the lemon into thin wedges and then crosswise into small dice, about ¼ cup.

2. Combine the diced lemon in a small bowl with the shallots, olives, basil, parsley, olive oil, and red pepper flakes. Taste and add salt, if needed.

sea bass "casino"-style

THIS BEAUTIFUL RETRO-STYLE entrée is a throwback to the once-popular appetizer, clams casino. Although we call for sea bass, this recipe is equally good made with halibut, striped bass, or snapper. We like it with mussels substituted for the clams, too. This dish has a lot complexity, but can be cooked in only a few minutes and with just one pan.

1 slice bacon

1 piece sea bass fillet (about 5 oz)

Salt and freshly ground pepper as needed

Flour as needed for dusting

2 tsp minced shallots

1 tbsp small-dice red pepper

1 tbsp small-dice green pepper

¼ cup dry white wine

5 littleneck or Manila clams

2 tsp lemon juice

1 tsp butter

1 tsp minced parsley

1. Cut the bacon in half lengthwise and then crosswise into ½-inch-wide pieces. Sauté the bacon over medium heat in a small non-stick skillet until browned and crisp, about 2 minutes. Remove the bacon bits with a slotted spoon, letting the fat drain back into the pan, and set aside to drain on a paper towel.

2. Return the skillet with the bacon fat to medium heat. Season the sea bass with salt and pepper, dust lightly with flour, and place it in the hot bacon fat. Cover the skillet and cook the sea bass until it is almost opaque in the center, turning once, about 3 minutes total cooking time. Transfer the fish to a plate.

3. Add the shallots and peppers to the skillet and sauté, stirring frequently, until the shallots are tender, about 30 seconds. Add the wine and clams and bring the wine to a boil. Cover the skillet and cook until the clams are just opened, about 5 minutes. Uncover and stir the lemon juice and butter into the pan juices. Add the fish and cook until just cooked through and hot, 1 or 2 minutes.

4. Place the sea bass and clams on a heated plate. Add the reserved bacon and the parsley to the pan juices; stir to combine. Taste the sauce and adjust the seasoning with salt and pepper, then spoon the sauce over and around the fish and clams.

CHICKEN WITH APPLES AND PRUNES

MARK: This is the type of dish you could prepare a day or two ahead of time, stopping short of adding the mustard and crème fraîche until you are ready to eat. It reheats well in the microwave or in a pot over very low heat. You might need to add a little water or stock to revive the sauce and keep everything moist.

LISA: We like to use chicken thighs for this dish because they stay moist even after simmering for some time in the sauce. The type of apple you choose really doesn't matter, but I tend to prefer an apple that is a bit tart and holds its shape, like Granny Smith or Jonagold. Any prunes left over from this dish make a delicious snack or dessert; sometimes I like them stuffed with a bit of dark chocolate and sprinkled with orange zest.

1 tsp canola oil, divided use

2 skinless chicken thighs

Salt and freshly ground pepper as needed

1 shallot, finely diced

1 tbsp finely diced pancetta or proscuitto

Pinch of minced fresh rosemary

¼ tsp chopped garlic

2 tbsp white wine

½ tsp white wine vinegar

⅓ cup Homemade Chicken Stock (page 134)

4 whole pitted prunes

½ apple, peeled and diced into ½-inch pieces

½ tsp whole grain mustard

1 tbsp crème fraîche, heavy cream or sour cream

1. Heat a small nonstick sauté pan with ½ teaspoon of canola oil over medium heat. Season the chicken with salt and pepper and add it to the pan. Sauté, turning once, until it is golden brown on both sides, 4 to 5 minutes total. Transfer the thighs to a plate.

2. Add the remaining ½ teaspoon canola oil to the pan and turn the heat to low. Add the shallot, pancetta, and rosemary. Cook, stirring frequently, until the shallot is soft and just starting to brown, about 2 minutes. Add the garlic and cook until fragrant, about 20 seconds.

3. Add the white wine and white wine vinegar. Simmer over medium heat until the liquid is very syrupy, about 2 minutes. Add the chicken stock and prunes; stir to dissolve the drippings. Return the chicken thighs and any juices they released to the pan. Cover and simmer over very low heat until the chicken is nearly cooked through, 6 to 7 minutes. Add the apple pieces and continue to cook until the chicken is cooked through and apples are tender, another 5 minutes.

4. Transfer the chicken to a dinner plate. Stir the mustard and crème fraîche into the sauce in the pan. Taste the sauce and adjust the seasoning with salt and pepper as needed. Pour the sauce over the chicken and serve.

buffalo salisbury steak

THIS RECIPE IS essentially just a dressed up hamburger. It would be delicious with Middle Eastern Carrots (page 110) and a multigrain pilaf. Ground buffalo is a healthier alternative to ground beef, although you can, of course, substitute ground beef or even ground turkey.

4 oz ground buffalo

1 scallion, minced

¼ tsp Worcestershire sauce

Pinch curry powder

Salt and freshly ground pepper as needed

½ tsp olive oil

4 mushrooms, thinly sliced

½ clove garlic, thinly sliced

1½ tsp red wine

1½ tsp Oven-dried Tomatoes (page 141) or sun-dried tomatoes, cut into slivers

¼ cup Homemade Chicken Stock (page 134)

1 tsp chopped and drained capers or fresh lemon juice

½ tsp chopped parsley

1. Mix together the buffalo, scallion, Worcestershire sauce, curry powder, salt, and pepper to taste. Mix the ingredients until they are just blended, being careful not to over mix. Shape into a patty about ¾ to 1 inch thick.

2. Heat the oil in a small sauté pan over medium heat. Add the patty and cook, turning once, until well-browned on both sides and cooked through, 6 to 8 minutes. Transfer the patty to a plate.

3. Return the pan to medium heat and add the mushrooms and garlic. Sauté until the mushrooms have released their juices and are browned, 3 or 4 minutes. Add the red wine and stir to release any drippings from the pan. Add the tomatoes and chicken stock and bring to a boil. Return the patty to the pan, reduce the heat to low, and simmer until the sauce has reduced and thickened slightly, about 2 minutes.

4. Remove the pan from the heat. Add the capers or lemon juice and chopped parsley to the sauce; stir to combine. Serve the patty on a heated plate and spoon the sauce over the meat.

braised lamb shanks with mashed potato and sautéed spinach

BRAISED LAMB SHANKS are comfort food at its best—succulent, creamy, and bursting with flavor. Although you could easily braise just one shank, it seems a shame not to take advantage of all that delicious sauce and braise a second shank at the same time. Like most braised dishes, this one freezes and reheats beautifully.

BRAISED LAMB SHANKS

SERVES 2

2 tsp olive oil

2 lamb shanks

Salt and freshly ground pepper

2 carrots, cut into 1½-inch pieces

½ small onion, diced small

4 cloves garlic, minced

2 tsp tomato paste

1 sprig fresh rosemary or ½ tsp dried

1 cup dry red wine

1½ cups Homemade Chicken Stock (page 134)

BREAD CRUMB TOPPING

½ cup bread crumbs

1 tbsp chopped parsley

1 tsp melted butter

½ tsp minced garlic

Mashed Potato (recipe follows)

Sautéed Spinach (page 86)

1. Preheat the oven to 325°F.

2. Heat the oil over medium heat in a Dutch oven large enough to comfortably fit the lamb without crowding. Season the lamb with salt and pepper, add it to the hot oil, and brown on all sides, turning as necessary, about 10 minutes total. Transfer the shanks to a plate.

3. Drain the excess fat from pan, leaving 1 teaspoon (enough to coat the pan). Return the pan to medium-low heat. Add the carrots, onion, and garlic and cook, stirring frequently, until the onion is golden, 3 to 5 minutes. Add the tomato paste and rosemary and continue cooking for another minute. Add the wine and stock and stir well to combine. Bring the liquid to a boil, and then return the lamb shanks to the pan.

4. Cover and braise in the oven until fork tender, about 2½ hours. Turn the shanks once or twice to keep them evenly moistened as they braise and adjust the oven temperature, if necessary, in order to maintain a very gentle simmer.

5. While the lamb is cooking, toss together the bread crumbs, parsley, butter, and garlic with a fork or your fingertips until evenly blended. Set aside.

6. When the lamb is fork tender, transfer it to a plate. Skim the fat from the sauce, taste, and season with salt and pepper. Return the lamb shanks to the sauce. At this point , the dish can be set aside to serve another day. Store the lamb and breadcrumbs separately. It can be refrigerated up to 3 days or frozen for up to 4 weeks.

7. When ready to serve, reheat the lamb, if necessary, in a covered pan over low heat on top of the stove, about 20 minutes, or in a baking dish in a 350°F oven until hot throughout, 30 to 40 minutes.

8. For each serving, spoon the mashed potatoes into a small casserole or gratin dish that can hold one shank comfortably. Place a lamb shank on top of the potatoes and spoon some of the vegetables around the lamb. Drizzle with ½ cup of braising liquid. Sprinkle half the bread crumb topping over each serving.

9. Preheat the oven to 350°F. Bake the lamb shank(s) until the bread crumb topping is browned, about 15 minutes. Serve the lamb shanks accompanied by sautéed spinach.

MASHED POTATO

1 russet potato

Salt and freshly ground pepper as needed

1 tbsp butter, room temperature

⅓ cup buttermilk, plus as needed

1. Peel the potato, cut it into medium dice, and place in a pot with enough cold water to cover by about 1 inch. Season the water with salt and bring it to a boil over medium-high heat. Reduce the heat to medium or low and simmer the potato until it is tender enough mash with a fork, about 12 minutes.

2. Drain the potato in a colander and return it to the same pot. Let the potato dry over low heat, shaking the pan occasionally, about 1 minute. Add the butter, and then use a fork or a potato masher to mash the butter into the potato until blended and creamy. Add half of the buttermilk and stir vigorously with a wooden spoon until light; adjust the consistency with additional buttermilk, and taste and season with salt and pepper.

southwestern beef stew

L IKE MOST BRAISES or stews, it seems more practical to make two servings, reserving one for another meal. Serve this stew with warm corn tortillas and a green salad with jícama, oranges, and red onion. You can substitute pork for the beef in this recipe. Carrots or other root vegetables can be substituted for or added to the potatoes. The stew can be made several days in advance and reheated when ready to serve, or can be frozen for up to 6 weeks without the potato.

SERVES 2

2 tsp canola oil, divided use

1½ tsp finely chopped garlic

⅔ cup chopped onion

2½ pasilla or ancho chiles, stemmed, seeds and veins removed

¾ cup water

1 cup Homemade Chicken Stock (page 134)

8 to 10 oz beef stew meat, cut into 1½-inch pieces

Salt and freshly ground pepper as needed

1 cup large-dice Yukon gold potato

Warmed corn tortillas (see note)

1. Preheat the oven to 325°F.

2. Heat ½ teaspoon of the canola oil in a small pot over medium-low heat. Add the garlic and onion and sauté, stirring frequently, until the onion is golden, about 5 minutes. Add the chiles and sauté until aromatic, about 1 minute. Add the water and stock and bring to boil. Reduce the heat to low and simmer until flavorful, 3 minutes. Remove from the heat, let it sit for 30 minutes to cool, and then puree it in a blender until smooth. Set the sauce aside.

3. Heat the remaining canola oil in a small Dutch oven over medium-high heat. Season the beef with salt and pepper and add it to the hot oil. Sauté until browned on all sides, turning the beef as necessary, about 6 minutes.

4. Add the reserved sauce and bring it to a boil. Cover the Dutch oven and place it in the oven for 45 minutes, adjusting the temperature as necessary to maintain a simmer. Add the potatoes, return the casserole to the oven, and cook until the potatoes are tender and the beef is very tender when pierced with a fork, another 25 to 35 minutes.

5. Remove the casserole from the oven and skim off any fat that has risen to the surface. Taste the stew and season with salt and pepper. Serve hot with warmed corn tortillas.

To warm tortillas, heat a small skillet over medium heat without any oil. Add the tortilla, and heat it on the first side until the tortilla softens and begins to blister a bit, about 30 seconds. Turn the tortilla and repeat on the second side. To keep tortillas warm, wrap them up in a clean napkin or towel.

grilled loin lamb chops with radicchio and red wine risotto

MARK: Here, radicchio is put to use in an unusual way. Its slight bitterness blends perfectly with the rich risotto and grilled meat.

LISA: In order to have everything ready to be served together, we partially cook the risotto and then set it aside while we grill the meat and radicchio. The last step is to finish the risotto while the chops are resting.

GRILLED LOIN LAMB CHOPS AND RADICCHIO

2 or 3 loin lamb chops (about 8 oz)

4 tsp olive oil, divided use

1 tbsp dry red wine

1 tsp minced rosemary

½ tsp minced garlic, divided use

¼ head radicchio, core intact, cut into 2 wedges

¼ tsp minced garlic

Salt and freshly ground pepper as needed

Radicchio and Red Wine Risotto (recipe follows)

1. Put the lamb chops in a zipper-close plastic bag. Add 3 teaspoons of the olive oil, the red wine, rosemary, and half of the garlic. Seal the bag, squeezing out the air, and then turn the bag a few times to coat the lamb evenly. Marinate in the refrigerator for at least 4 and up to 24 hours.

2. Mix the remaining ½ teaspoon olive oil with ¼ teaspoon minced garlic and a pinch of salt and pepper and brush over the radicchio wedges.

3. Preheat a grill to medium-high. Remove the lamb chops from the marinade and season with salt and pepper. Grill the chops over direct heat on the first side until they are browned and about halfway cooked, 3 to 4 minutes. Grill the radicchio over medium direct heat until tender and slightly charred, about 4 minutes total. Turn the chops and finish grilling until cooked to the desired degree of doneness, another 2 or 3 minutes for medium-rare. Transfer the chops to a plate to rest. Cut the radicchio into ½-inch-wide strips and set aside to add to the risotto (below).

RADICCHIO AND RED WINE RISOTTO

2 tsp unsalted butter, divided use

2 tbsp finely chopped onion

3 tbsp Arborio rice

3 tbsp red wine

1 cup Homemade Chicken Stock (page 134), boiling

2 tsp grated Parmesan

Grilled radicchio, reserved from preceding recipe

1. Melt 1 teaspoon of butter over medium-low heat in a small heavy bottomed saucepan. Add the onion and sauté until softened and slightly browned, 3 to 4 minutes. Add the rice and cook, stirring constantly, until the rice is slightly parched and smells of popcorn, about 2 minutes.

2. Add the wine and bring to a simmer, stirring constantly, until the wine has been absorbed by the rice, about 3 minutes. Add ¼ cup of the chicken stock and cook, stirring constantly, until the rice absorbs the stock, another 4 minutes. Add another ¼ cup of the stock and cook until it is absorbed, about 4 minutes, and then repeat with another ¼ cup of stock. (Pull the pot off the heat now while you grill the lamb chops and radicchio.)

3. Add the final ¼ cup of chicken stock and cook, stirring constantly, until the rice is tender, but still has some texture, another 4 minutes. The risotto should have a creamy, porridge-like consistency.

4. Remove the pan from the heat and stir in the reserved radicchio strips, the remaining 1 tsp of butter, and the Parmesan. Taste and season with salt and pepper, if needed. Serve the risotto immediately along with the grilled lamb chops.

caramelized pineapple with black peppercorns and ice cream

LISA: This is one of Mark's recipes from when he worked in Switzerland many years ago. It always elicits surprise—and then pleasure—from those who try it.

MARK: You can vary the ice cream and the liquor used to suit your taste. Try green or pink peppercorns if you prefer a milder flavor.

1 tbsp granulated sugar

¼ tsp black pepper, coarsely crushed

1 ring fresh pineapple, about ½ inch thick

¼ cup orange juice

1 tbsp Kirsch or rum

Vanilla ice cream

1. Mix together the sugar and black pepper. Sprinkle the mixture on both sides of the pineapple.

2. Heat a small nonstick skillet over high heat. When the pan is hot, add the pineapple and let it cook, without disturbing, until the sugar begins to caramelize around the edges of the pineapple, 2 or 3 minutes.

3. Add 1 tablespoon of the orange juice and swirl the pan to mix the juice with the caramelized sugar as it reduces to a syrup. Continue adding the juice, a bit at a time, as the pineapple continues to cook and caramelize, about 2 minutes. Turn the pineapple over and repeat on the second side. When both sides are brown and glazed, add the Kirsch or rum and reduce. Add any remaining orange juice, swirling the pan to blend the sauce.

4. Serve the pineapple on a plate, spoon the caramelized syrup over the pineapple, and top with a scoop of ice cream in the center of the pineapple ring.

chocolate fondue

LISA: This "special treat" dessert takes very little effort to put together. There are many fresh and dried fruits that pair well with chocolate. Use what you have at home and experiment with something different each time. The fondue can be made ahead and refrigerated. Rewarm it in the microwave, being carefully not to overheat it.

MARK: Milk or semisweet chocolate can be substituted for the bittersweet chocolate called for here. Use the best quality you can buy. We prefer Valrhona. The candied ginger adds a nice bite. However, it can be left out completely or substituted with finely chopped nuts or candied orange zest.

1 tbsp heavy cream or whole milk

1 oz high-quality bittersweet chocolate, chopped

½ tsp finely chopped candied ginger, optional

Pieces of fresh fruit and or cake

1. Combine the cream or milk and the chocolate in an individual soufflé dish or small microwavable cup. Microwave on high for a few seconds, until the cream is hot and the chocolate is beginning to melt.

2. Remove the dish and stir the mixture until it is glossy and smooth. Stir in the ginger, if using. Serve the fondue warm with pieces of fresh fruit and or cake, using a small skewer or fork to dip the fruit into the chocolate.

icebox cookies

LISA: This is one simple cookie recipe with four different flavorings. The dough freezes well, so you can bake a few cookies at a time, indulging yourself on a moment's notice.

MARK: The mix-ins listed in this recipe can be varied according to your taste. The cornstarch keeps the cookies crisp, and also makes the dough very easy to handle.

1 cup unsalted butter, at room temperature

½ cup sugar

1¾ cups flour

⅓ cup cornstarch

¼ tsp salt

MIX-IN OPTIONS: (AMOUNTS SHOWN WILL FLAVOR ¼ RECIPE)

Option 1: 1½ tsp finely chopped thyme (lemon thyme is best)

Option 2: 1 tsp citrus zest, (mix of lemon, lime, orange), ¼ tsp orange flower water (optional)

Option 3: ½ tsp vanilla and ¼ cup unsweetened shredded coconut

Option 4: ½ tsp cinnamon, pinch each of ground cloves and nutmeg, 2 tbsp toasted chopped walnuts or pecans

1. Process the butter and sugar together in a food processor until light, about 1½ minutes. Add the flour, cornstarch, and salt and process until the mixture is just combined, about 25 seconds.

2. Divide the dough into four small bowls. Add a "mix-in" to each bowl, stirring well to combine. Shape the dough into logs that are about 1½ inches thick. Wrap each log individually in plastic or waxed paper. Refrigerate at least 2 hours before slicing and baking them (or freeze them for up to 8 weeks).

4. Preheat the oven to 325°F. Line cookie sheets with parchment or silicone liner.

5. Unwrap the logs and slice the cookie dough into rounds about ¼ inch thick. Place the rounds on lined cookie sheets and bake until the edges of the cookies are just slightly browned, 20 to 25 minutes.

HOMEMADE CHICKEN STOCK

WHILE THERE ARE many different stocks used in cooking, in this cookbook we are offering a recipe for just one that can be used with everything unless, of course, you are a vegetarian. Chicken stock is simple, versatile, and can be made in advance. Homemade stock makes an enormous difference in the taste of a dish, resulting in cleaner and fresher flavors. We don't add salt to our stock because we know we'll be seasoning the dish that contains the stock.

Chicken stock is a basic ingredient used in many recipes. Fortunately, it is also easy to make and forgiving if you do not follow the recipe exactly. At its best, it is made with an old stewing fowl, cooked slowly for hours with vegetables, herbs, and spices, which results in a stock full of flavor and a gelatinous body when chilled. However, when pressed for time or being just plain lazy (yes, it happens to professional chefs, too), we have been known to make a quick version using a few bones or meat, no vegetables or spices. While these shortcuts might not yield the perfect stock, it is still superior to most of the canned products purchased at grocery stores.

Although the cooking time for stock is long, it requires very little hands-on work. No time to attend to the stock? You can put together all of the ingredients and then make it on a weekend or in the evening while preparing dinner. It can be refrigerated partway through the cooking process and finished another day, if necessary. Often, because of time constraints, we cook and chill it one day, and then the next day bring it back to a boil and strain it.

Once you've cooked, strained, and cooled the stock, pour it into different sized freezer containers ranging from ½ cup to 2 cups or so. You could also freeze the stock in ice cube trays; one cube equals about 2 tablespoons.

MAKES 2½ QUARTS

2½ lb chicken parts or bones, rinsed

5 qts cold water

1 large carrot, large dice

1 stalk celery, large dice

1 onion, large dice

4 parsley sprigs

5 thyme sprigs

1 bay leaf

10 whole peppercorns

1. In a large stockpot, bring the chicken and water to a boil over high heat. Skim the fat and foam from the surface with a spoon, reduce the heat to low and simmer slowly, partially covered, for 2 hours. Continue to skim any fat or foam that rises to the surface from time to time. Add the remaining ingredients and simmer 1 more hour.

2. Strain the stock through a fine sieve, pressing on the solids to extract as much liquid as possible. The stock is ready to use now, or it may be cooled and then stored in containers in the refrigerator for up to 5 days or in the freezer for up to 3 months.

TOMATO SAUCE

LISA: I come from a family of great home cooks and we all have gardens. We would never buy jarred tomato sauce when the summer's bounty always provides more than enough sauce to get us through the winter. We all love a shortcut, so when one full-time working sister came up with a roasted tomato sauce that required minimum effort and attention, we were instant converts. This recipe has become the yearly standard in everyone's repertoire. Hopefully, you'll feel the same.

This is the tomato sauce to make when summer tomatoes are plentiful. It's forgiving with ingredients and quantities. I use whatever garden tomatoes I have waiting to be used up, which can be a mixture of plum, beefsteak, and cherry. The variety doesn't matter because roasting the tomatoes keeps the sauce from being watery. Sometimes I will even add a carrot if I want more of a roasted vegetable flavor.

MAKES 2 CUPS

2 lb cored and quartered tomatoes

½ onion, peeled and sliced (about 4 oz)

2 garlic cloves, peeled and coarsely chopped

2 tbsp olive oil

4 basil leaves, optional

Salt and freshly ground pepper as needed

Pinch of sugar, optional

1. Preheat the oven to 350°F. Toss the tomatoes, onion, garlic, and olive oil together in an 8" × 13" roasting pan. Roast, uncovered, for 1 hour, stirring occasionally to break up the tomatoes. Add the basil leaves, if using. Roast for another 15 minutes. Remove from the oven and cool to room temperature. Some of the vegetables will be browned in spots, which adds a nice, rich flavor.

2. Pass the vegetables through a food mill or process them in a food processor until puréed, then strain through a medium sieve, pressing on the solids, to remove the skin and seeds. Season to taste with salt and pepper and a pinch of sugar if the sauce seems too acidic.

3. Heat the sauce over low heat and combine with cooked pasta, or store the sauce in jars in the refrigerator for up to 1 week or in freezer containers for up to 6 months.

PREPARING DRIED LEGUMES

Dried legumes are easy to prepare and have a better texture than the canned product. Cooking your own also enables you to cut back on the sodium content, which can be quite high in many canned foods.

One of the most common mistakes in preparing beans is undercooking them. When properly cooked they should be completely tender, not crunchy. Do not be alarmed if a few of the beans in the pot have broken into pieces and lost their shape. That is natural. However, once drained and cooled, you will notice that most of the beans are still whole, and that they have a better texture than most canned beans.

Our recipe makes a large batch of legumes, as there are several recipes in the book which use them. They last beautifully stored in the refrigerator or the freezer.

BASIC BEAN RECIPE

ABOUT 5 CUPS

1 lb dried beans

Cold water as needed

1 large garlic clove, crushed

3 thyme sprigs

1 bay leaf

Salt as needed

1. Sprt the beans, put them in a large bowl and add enough cold water to cover them by 3 or 4 inches. Swish the beans; remove and discard any beans that float on the surface. Drain the beans and replace the water. Let the beans soak at least 4 and up to 24 hours (depending upon the type of bean; see the table opposite).

2. Drain the beans in a colander and then place them in a large pot with enough fresh water to cover by 3 to 4 inches. Add the garlic, thyme, and bay leaf and bring to a boil over high heat. Skim the foam from the surface.

3. Reduce the heat to low and simmer, partially covered, until tender (see the table opposite for cooking times), skimming the foam as needed. Season with salt after the beans are tender. The beans are ready to drain and use now, or you may let them cool in their cooking liquid and then store them in covered containers in the refrigerator for 3 or 4 days or in the freezer for up to 4 months. Remove and discard the garlic, thyme sprigs, and bay leaf prior to storing.

STEAMED AND SIMMERED GRAINS

The table opposite lists some of the grains that we love to include in our meals. Some grains may require rinsing and soaking before you cook them.

APPROXIMATE SOAKING AND COOKING TIMES FOR SELECTED LEGUMES

TYPE	SOAKING TIME	COOKING TIME	YIELD, 1 CUP DRY
Black beans	4 hours	1½ hours	3 cups
Black-eyed peas	*	1 hour	2½ cups
Chickpeas	4 hours	2 to 2½ hours	3 cups
Fava beans	12 hours	3 hours	3 cups
Great Northern beans	4 hours	1 hour	2¾ cups
Kidney beans (red or white)	4 hours	1 hour	2¾ cups
Lentils	*	30 to 40 minutes	3 cups
Lima beans	4 hours	1 to 1½ hours	3 cups
Mung beans	4 hours	1 hour	3 cups
Navy beans	4 hours	2 hours	2¾ cups
Pink beans	4 hours	1 hour	3 cups
Pinto beans	4 hours	1 to 1½ hours	3¼ cups

*Soaking is not necessary.

APPROXIMATE COOKING TIMES FOR SELECTED GRAINS

GRAIN	MEASURE	LIQUID	COOKING TIME
White rice	¼ cup	¾ cup	12 minutes
Jasmine rice	¼ cup	¾ cup	12 minutes
Brown rice	¼ cup	¾ cup	25 minutes
Farro	¼ cup	¾ cup	25 minutes
Bulgur	¼ cup	¾ cup	8 minutes
Couscous	¼ cup	¾ cup	5 minutes
Quinoa	¼ cup	¾ cup	12 minutes
Barley	¼ cup	¾ cup	35 minutes

The basic steps involved in steaming or simmering a grain are these:

Measure the grain and pour it into a saucepot that has a tight-fitting lid. Use a 1-quart pot to make 1 or 2 portions.

Measure the appropriate amount of a cold liquid—almost invariably water. Add enough salt to the water to make it taste just barely salty.

Put the pot over high heat and bring the water to a boil. Stir the grain a few times to keep the individual kernels from sticking together.

Once the water is boiling, cover the pot tightly, reduce the heat to low, and let the grain cook undisturbed until it is tender to the bite. (Couscous is added to boiling water, covered, and left to absorb the liquid off the heat.) Fluff cooked grains with a fork; if you stir them with a spoon, they can mash together.

SALAD DRESSINGS

BOTTLED DRESSINGS MASK the flavor of a salad. With the fabulous selections of lettuces on the market today, it would be a shame not to do them justice.

CLASSIC VINAIGRETTE

THIS IS A traditional salad dressing, one we like to serve with the delicate mescluns, although it really works well with any greens. This vinaigrette will easily keep one week in the refrigerator if you remove the smashed garlic before storing.

1 tbsp minced shallots

1 tbsp red wine vinegar

1 tbsp sherry vinegar

Sea salt and freshly ground pepper as needed

½ clove garlic, smashed

½ tsp Dijon mustard

⅓ cup olive oil

Macerate the shallots in a bowl with the vinegars and a large pinch of salt. Let stand for 5 minutes to soften the harshness of the onion flavor. Add the garlic and Dijon. Slowly whisk in the olive oil and season to taste with salt and the pepper. The vinaigrette is ready to use now or it may be stored in a covered jar in the refrigerator for up to 1 week.

BALSAMIC VINAIGRETTE

THIS IS A versatile salad dressing which works with most lettuces and many vegetables. The shallots and garlic stand up well to the bold flavor of the vinegar. For a different flavor, try dijon mustard instead of whole grain.

1 tbsp finely chopped shallots

2½ tbsp balsamic vinegar

1 tsp mustard, preferably whole grain

½ tsp finely chopped garlic

⅓ cup olive oil

Salt and freshly ground pepper as needed

Place the shallots in a bowl with the vinegar. Macerate for 5 minutes. Whisk in the remaining ingredients and season to taste with salt and pepper. The vinaigrette is ready to use now or it may be stored in a covered jar in the refrigerator for up to 1 week.

WALNUT OIL VINAIGRETTE

THERE ARE MANY different brands of walnut oil on the market—some have a very faint walnut flavor and others are quite pronounced. For this dressing, use one with full flavor. It will sometimes be listed as "toasted walnut oil." Depending on the pungency of the oil, you may need to adjust the amount of canola oil you use in the recipe. Keep the opened bottle of walnut oil in the refrigerator and use it up within 6 months. For variety, try this vinaigrette made with raspberry vinegar instead of red wine vinegar.

2 tsp finely chopped shallots

2 tbsp red wine vinegar

2 tbsp walnut oil

2 tbsp canola oil

¾ tsp Dijon mustard

Salt and freshly ground pepper as needed

Place the shallots in a small bowl. Add the vinegar and a pinch of salt and pepper. Let this macerate for 5 minutes. Whisk in the remaining ingredients and season to taste with salt and pepper. The vinaigrette is ready to use now or it may be stored in a covered container in the refrigerator for up to 1 week.

LEMON-GARLIC SALAD DRESSING

THIS HAS BEEN the standard salad dressing in our house for many years—fresh tasting and versatile. For the best dressing, use good quality extra-virgin olive oil and freshly squeezed lemon juice. Add herbs or chopped shallots for additional flavor.

½ clove garlic, peeled

½ tsp Dijon mustard

2 tbsp fresh lemon juice

4 tbsp extra virgin olive oil

Salt and freshly ground pepper as needed

Smash the garlic clove by pressing on it hard with the flat side of your knife blade. Mash the garlic against the surface of a small bowl with a table fork. Add the mustard and lemon juice. Slowly whisk in the oil. Taste and season with salt and pepper. Remove any large garlic pieces before serving or storing. The dressing can be refrigerated for up to 1 week.

GREEK SALAD DRESSING

THIS DRESSING CAN be used with a variety of tossed green salads in addition to the traditional romaine typically used in a Greek salad. Try it with hardy winter greens such as radicchio, Belgian endive, and chicory. It can also be drizzled over summer tomatoes or used as a marinade for chicken or lamb.

¼ clove garlic

Salt and freshly ground pepper as needed

1 tsp dried oregano

3 tbsp red wine vinegar

¼ tsp Dijon mustard

6 tbsp extra virgin olive oil

Mash the garlic with a bit of salt. Combine the mashed garlic with the oregano, vinegar, and mustard in a bowl. Slowly whisk in olive oil. Season with salt and pepper to taste. The dressing is ready to use now or it may be stored in a covered jar in the refrigerator for up to 1 week.

SHAVED PARMESAN CURLS

We buy chunks of Parmesan cheese so we can cut away very thin slices, or curls. Instead of a knife, use a vegetable peeler to make the cuts so thin that they curl.

PESTO

LISA: This recipe varies a bit from traditional pesto with the addition of parsley and chicken stock. The parsley adds a milder flavor to the peppery bite of basil and the chicken stock substitutes for some of the oil, resulting in a lighter sauce with fewer calories. I always make pesto in the the food processor. It's so quick and, in this recipe, I like the way it emulsifies the chicken stock with the oil. I never freeze pesto and will only eat it the day it is made.

MARK: When I make pesto, I follow the traditional method that calls for making it in a mortar and pestle, which works well for a recipe making a small amount, such as this one. I do not add the cheese until adding the pesto to a dish because I prefer to add Parmesan to the dish rather than to the pesto. That way, I add only what I want, if any, and it does not stick to the bowl or spoon when it gets hot. I add a little extra salt to help keep the color green. It freezes better that way, as well. My "make and freeze" strategy is widely accepted in many homes, particularly those with a garden. Even if we don't agree about the virtues of frozen pesto, we do agree that homemade pesto is so easy to make that neither one of us would ever buy it ready-made.

LISA'S PESTO

MAKES ²/₃ CUP

½ large garlic clove, peeled

2 tbsp toasted pine nuts or walnuts

¼ tsp salt

½ cup parsley leaves

²/₃ cup basil leaves

¼ cup finely grated Parmesan cheese

2 tbsp Homemade Chicken Stock (page 134)

¼ cup olive oil

Salt and freshly ground pepper as needed

1. Combine the garlic, pine nuts, and salt in the bowl of a small food processor. Process

until finely chopped, scraping down the sides occasionally.

2. Add the parsley and basil; process again until the herbs are chopped fine. Scrape down the sides and add the Parmesan.

3. With the food processor motor running, slowly add the chicken stock and olive oil, processing until emulsified. Season with salt and pepper.

MARK'S PESTO

MAKES ½ CUP

1 cup packed basil leaves

½ garlic clove, peeled

½ tsp kosher salt

3 tbsp toasted pine nuts

6 tbsp extra-virgin olive oil, plus as needed for storing

Grated Parmesan cheese, as needed

1. Chop the basil leaves and garlic with a knife into coarse pieces.

2. Add the basil, garlic, and salt to a mortar and pestle. Pound and grind the ingredients with the pestle until a relatively even, but still coarse, paste develops. Add the pine nuts and continue to grind together until they are evenly blended into the mixture.

3. Add the olive oil a tablespoon at a time, mixing the oil in with the pestle as you add it. The pesto should be dense and creamy.

4. Transfer the pesto to a bowl or a jar. To store the pesto, let it settle for a few minutes

so the oil can rise to the top and cover the basil. If necessary, pour additional oil over the surface of the pesto to cover it. Store in a covered container in the refrigerator for up to 2 days, or freeze for up to 8 weeks. Add the Parmesan to the pesto as desired before using.

OVEN-DRIED TOMATOES

THIS IS A good way to use up extra cherry tomatoes during gardening season or a great sale at the market. We prefer our home-made recipe to purchased sun-dried tomatoes. They have a fresh flavor and a pleasant texture. Once dried, they keep in the refrigerator for several weeks.

These take a long time to cook, but the low oven temperature means they require very little attention; you can do whatever you need to with just periodic checks. The low heat and long cooking time dries out the tomatoes while slowly caramelizing them.

MAKES ABOUT ¾ CUP

1 pint cherry tomatoes, halved

2 tbsp olive oil

2 cloves garlic, thinly sliced

7 large sprigs fresh thyme

Sea salt and freshly ground pepper as needed

1. Preheat the oven to 225°F.

2. Toss the tomatoes together with the oil, garlic, and thyme on a shallow baking sheet. Season with salt and pepper. Turn the tomatoes so the cut side is facing up. Bake until dried but still slightly soft and starting to caramelize, 2½ to 3½ hours.

3. Allow the tomatoes to cool to room temperature, then remove and discard the thyme sprigs. Pack the tomatoes in containers and cover tightly. They will last 3 weeks in the refrigerator.

MAKING CITRUS FRUIT SEGMENTS AND ZEST

To make citrus segments that don't have any bits of membrane or pit, make two slices that take off the top and bottom of the citrus fruit. With one of the cut sides facing down, use a paring knife to trim away the skin and the white pith just below it. Hold the fruit in one hand over a bowl so you can collect the fruit and the juices. Use a paring knife to cut the membranes away from the segements. As you cut, the segments will drop into the bowl.

To make long strips of zest, use a vegetable peeler or sharp knife to cut away long pieces. Lay the pieces flat on a work surface; use a knife to carefully remove the bitter white pith, then cut the zest into long, thin strips (julienne) with a chef's knife.

PIZZA DOUGH

W E LIKE THE taste and texture of this dough, which is made with equal parts of white and light whole wheat flours. If you have trouble finding light whole wheat flour, use 1¼ cups of regular whole wheat flour and 2¾ cups of white flour instead.

MAKES 5 PORTIONS, ABOUT 6 OZ EACH

1 package yeast

1½ cups warm water (about 110°F)

3 tbsp olive oil

2 cups all purpose white flour

2 cups light whole wheat flour

1½ tsp salt

1. In a small bowl, stir the yeast into ½ cup of the warm water. Let sit for 5 minutes until dissolved.

2. Combine the remaining 1 cup warm water with olive oil. Set aside.

3. Combine the flours and salt in the bowl of a food processor and pulse the machine once or twice to blend. With the machine running, add the yeast mixture along with the water-olive oil mixture to the flour. Process until a ball forms. Scrape down the sides of the bowl and process 40 seconds longer to knead.

4. Transfer the dough to a floured surface and knead it by hand until the dough is satiny and smooth, dusting the dough and work surface with additional flour, if necessary, about 3 minutes.

5. Place the dough in an oiled bowl, preferably one with straight sides, cover, and let rise in a warm place until doubled, about 1 hour.

6. Turn the dough out onto a floured surface and divide it into 5 equal pieces (about 6 oz each). Round the dough into tight balls, cover with a towel, and let sit for 20 to 30 minutes.

7. The dough is ready to be baked now or it may be wrapped tightly and stored in the refrigerator for up to 8 hours or in the freezer for 2 months. To thaw the dough, take it from the freezer and place it in the refrigerator, still wrapped, for about 8 hours.

MAKE YOUR OWN FROZEN PIZZA

Instead of freezing the dough in balls, you can shape the dough (see page 39). Add any toppings you like and bake the pizza just until the crust is set, but not browned, 5 to 6 minutes. Then, let the pizza cool to room temperature, wrap well, and freeze. Bake the pizza directly from the freezer for about 12 minutes.

PÂTE BRISÈE

MAKE A BATCH of this all-purpose dough for sweet and savory pies and tarts. You can use half now, then freeze the rest for the future. This recipe makes enough for two individual crusts.

This recipe is easy to mix by hand, but you could also make it in a small food processor, pulsing the machine on and off to cut in the butter. It is best to then transfer it to a bowl so you can add the water by hand. It is easier to judge how much water needs to be added and avoid overmixing the dough.

MAKES 2 PORTIONS, ABOUT 2½ OUNCES EACH

½ cup all purpose flour

2 tbsp cold unsalted butter

1 tbsp cold or frozen shortening

¼ tsp salt

2 tbsp ice cold water, use as needed

1. Place the flour, butter, shortening, and salt in a bowl. Cut the butter and shortening into the flour until it is the size of peas. Add 4 teaspoons of water and stir lightly with a fork until it just starts to form moist clumps, adding a bit more water, if necessary.

2. Divide the dough into 2 portions and wrap them individually with plastic wrap. Chill the dough at least 30 minutes before rolling as directed in your recipe. The dough will last up to 3 days in the refrigerator or 5 months in the freezer. Thaw it gently by leaving it in the refrigerator overnight.

GRILLED COUNTRY-STYLE BREAD

To make grilled bread, rub or brush a slice of a good bread with olive oil. Grill the bread over medium heat (or under the broiler), turning once, until golden brown, 1 or 2 minutes per side. Cut a garlic clove in half and rub the cut sides on the bread.

QUICK PUFF PASTRY

THIS RECIPE IS an easy version of classic puff pastry. It is ideal for tarts and desserts that require a flaky crust, but do not need to rise high like a filled puff pastry dessert. It is also much easier to roll out and can be made in a shorter time. We always keep a batch on hand, frozen in small portions, for last minute desserts. It is far superior to the store bought product. A few hints to ensure success with this recipe:

- Make sure the butter is frozen as directed in the recipe.

- Work quickly when rolling and folding the dough to keep the butter cool and prevent it from softening and becoming sticky.

- If the dough becomes too sticky or tough to roll, dust it with flour and let it rest for an hour in the refrigerator before continuing.

MAKES ABOUT 2 POUNDS, OR 10 INDIVIDUAL PORTIONS

3 cups all purpose flour

1 tsp salt

1²⁄₃ cups cubed butter, frozen

1 cup ice water

1. Combine the flour and salt in the bowl of a food processor. Add the frozen butter and process until the butter is chopped to small bits, about ¼ inch or the size of peas. Transfer the dough to a bowl. Add the water and toss briefly to combine.

2. Turn the dough out onto floured surface. Roll it into a rectangle that measures 16 inches long, 9 inches wide, and ½ inch thick. Avoid rolling over the edge of the dough and try to keep the edges straight and the corners square. At this point, the dough will look rough and lumpy.

3. Fold the dough in thirds, the way you would fold a letter. Turn the dough 90 degrees so the long end is parallel to the edge of the work surface. Roll the dough out a second time to the same dimensions, fold it in thirds once more, and turn the dough 90 degrees.

4. Roll and fold the dough in this manner twice more, for a total of four folds. By now the dough should be smooth.

5. Put the dough on a baking sheet, cover it with plastic wrap, and refrigerate for an hour. Roll and fold two more times.

6. Wrap the dough and let it chill until firm, about 1 hour. At this point the dough is ready to be cut into 10 pieces (3-oz pieces are good for individual tarts and galettes). It will keep in the refrigerator for 3 days or 4 to 5 months in the freezer.

USING A STOVE TOP GRILL

A heavy-gauge grill pan gives foods the same distinctive marks and some of the smokiness we enjoy in grilled foods. Grill pans have raised ridges that simulate the rods on a charcoal or gas grill. Choose a pan that fits over a single burner and that is made from cast iron since that metal can get and stay very hot. Preheat the griddle over direct heat until it is hot. Spray or rub it with a little cooking oil to prevent your food from sticking.

DIRECT AND INDIRECT GRILLING

CONTROLLING THE TEMPERATURE of the grill as foods cook is one of the challenges facing the outdoor chef. Using direct or indirect grilling techniques (or a combination of the two) gives you the flexibility to prepare almost any food on the grill, even large cuts of meat or delicate fruits.

Direct-heat grilling means that foods are placed directly over a lively flame or bed of coals, where the heat is highest and foods cook quickly. This is perfect for small portions like thin steaks or chicken breasts. Indirect-heat grilling means that foods are placed on part of the grill close to, but not directly over, the heat source. The heat is less intense there, so foods that take longer to cook (such as spareribs) or that might scorch (pizza or vegetables) can finish cooking without turning black.

TESTING THE TEMPERATURE OF YOUR GRILL

Some grills have built-in thermometers that make it easy to monitor how hot the grill is. If you don't have swuch a feature on your grill, you can use a time-honored test:

Hold your hand, palm facing down, over the heat source just above the grill rack. Count how many seconds it takes before you have to take your hand away from the grill.

- 2 seconds equals high heat
- 3 seconds equals medium-high heat
- 4 seconds equals medium heat
- 5 seconds equals medium-low heat
- 6 seconds equals low heat

MAKING A CHARCOAL FIRE

A GOOD FIRE burns evenly and lasts long enough to cook everything completely. Our preference is to grill over hardwood charcoal. It's all natural, lights quickly, and burns hot. While gas grills may take as little as 15 minutes to heat up, a charcoal fire typically takes 20 to 35 minutes before it is ready for cooking. We strongly recommend avoiding using lighter fluid and treated charcoal briquettes, which can leave a distinct flavor on foods. Never use gasoline or kerosene to start a fire.

INDEX

A Note on the Type

The text of this book was set in the OpenType
version of Goudy Oldstyle, the eponymous typeface of
the American type designer, Frederic Goudy, as released
in digital form by the new Lanston Type Company. The
typeface was originally issued by the American Type
Founders in 1915, and later adapted by Goudy
for use on the Monotype machine.

Art direction, design, and composition by Kevin Hanek

Printed in Thailand by Imago